About Island Press

Since 1984, the nonprofit organization Island Press has been stimulating, shaping, and communicating ideas that are essential for solving environmental problems worldwide. With more than 800 titles in print and some 40 new releases each year, we are the nation's leading publisher on environmental issues. We identify innovative thinkers and emerging trends in the environmental field. We work with world-renowned experts and authors to develop cross-disciplinary solutions to environmental challenges.

Island Press designs and executes educational campaigns in conjunction with our authors to communicate their critical messages in print, in person, and online using the latest technologies, innovative programs, and the media. Our goal is to reach targeted audiences—scientists, policymakers, environmental advocates, urban planners, the media, and concerned citizens—with information that can be used to create the framework for long-term ecological health and human well-being.

Island Press gratefully acknowledges major support of our work by The Agua Fund, The Andrew W. Mellon Foundation, Betsy & Jesse Fink Foundation, The Bobolink Foundation, The Curtis and Edith Munson Foundation, Forrest C. and Frances H. Lattner Foundation, G.O. Forward Fund of the Saint Paul Foundation, Gordon and Betty Moore Foundation, The JPB Foundation, The Kresge Foundation, The Margaret A. Cargill Foundation, New Mexico Water Initiative, a project of Hanuman Foundation, The Overbrook Foundation, The S.D. Bechtel, Jr. Foundation, The Summit Charitable Foundation, Inc., V. Kann Rasmussen Foundation, The Wallace Alexander Gerbode Foundation, and other generous supporters.

The opinions expressed in this book are those of the author(s) and do not necessarily reflect the views of our supporters.

Future Arctic

Future Arctic

Field Notes from a World on the Edge

Edward Struzik

ISLANDPRESS

Washington | Covelo | London

Library of Congress Control Number: 2014948287

Printed on recycled, acid-free paper ⊛

Manufactured in the United States of America
10 9 8 7 6 5 4 3 2 1

Keywords: Arctic Council, Peace-Athabasca delta, avian cholera, Bering Sea,
British Columbia, cackling goose, Canada goose, caribou, Chinchaga fire,
Chukchi Sea, Churchill, cod, Ellef Ringnes, *Exxon Valdez*, Greenland,
grizzly bear, Hudson Bay, hybridization, Ice Age, Inuit, Mackenzie delta,
narwhal, Norwegian Polar Institute, ocean current, orca, peregrine falcon,
polar bear, salmon, Shishmaref, snow goose, snowy owl, Svalbard,
Tuktoyaktuk, wolf, wood bison, Yukon Territory

To my wife, Julia, and to my children, Jacob and Sigrid,
who have participated in a number of my Arctic expeditions.
Those are the journeys north that I treasure most.

To the people who live in the Arctic, my thanks for
your hospitality and for sharing your insights.

Contents

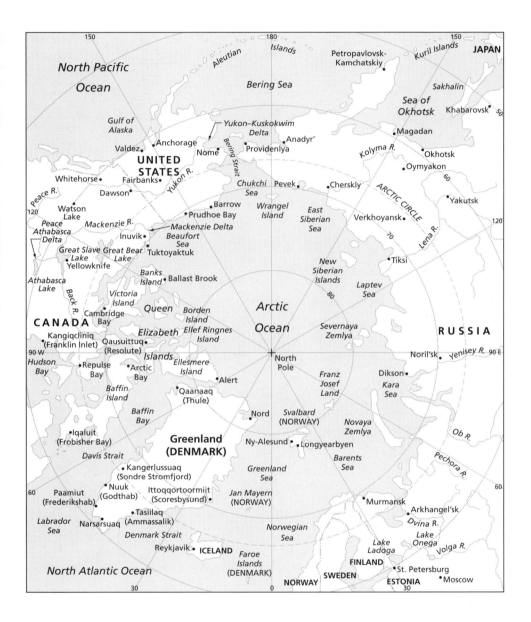

Introduction

THE BEGINNING OF WHAT many people thought was the end of the world began on June 2, 1950, when a small wildfire ignited in the boreal forest in northern British Columbia near the Yukon border and the Chinchaga River.

It had been an exceptionally hot spring, and forest firefighters were too busy battling other fires to do anything about a little fire like this one, which was remote and far from human settlement. Within a few days, though, it crossed into the largely uninhabited wildlands of northern Alberta. Fueled by a tinder-dry forest that went on forever, the relatively small blaze developed into a wildfire of such monstrous proportions that the thickness of the smoke led some people in southern Canada, the United States, and Europe to believe that an atomic bomb had exploded and that the western world was at war with the Soviet Union.

It was not an alien invasion, a volcanic eruption, or an eclipse of the sun as others suspected. At one point, though, flights in the United States and Canada had to be canceled, including one that was searching for a downed U.S. bomber in northern Ontario. In Buffalo, Pittsburgh, Cleveland, Fort Erie, and many towns in New York, it was so dark at midday that the lights at baseball fields, including those at

Yankee Stadium, had to be turned on to illuminate the playing fields. Smoke from the Canadian fire could be detected as far away as Europe. Some Danes were so "jittery" when they woke up to see a blue sun rising over the horizon that they went to the bank to withdraw their life savings.

It wasn't only people that reacted to the dark pall of smoke that hung in the sky. In an article in a Jamestown, New York, newspaper, a farmer described how his chickens, which had fanned out for their midday foraging, "suddenly realized they were being caught by darkness, so they scurried back across the cow yard in more than usual earnest, their heads moving in delayed jerks."

All told, the Chinchaga fire of 1950 burned for 222 days and torched a stretch of forest that was 175 miles long and more than 3.5 million acres in size. Astronomer Carl Sagan was so intrigued that he inquired to see how it might be used to describe his concept of a "nuclear winter."

Fast-forward to the exceptionally warm summers in Alaska and the Yukon Territory in 2004, 2007, and 2014 when three other remarkable fire seasons unfolded.

I remember the 2004 fire season all too well because it forced me to cancel a family visit and a canoe trip down the Wind River in the Yukon. A record 1.5 million hectares were torched in the territory that year. Another 2.7 million hectares of forest burned in neighboring Alaska. Together they burned an area the size of Massachusetts and New Hampshire combined. Smoke from the fires could be detected all the way to the east coast of Canada and throughout many parts of the contiguous United States. Traffic on parts of the Alaska Highway was shut down for days at a time. Alaskans suffered for fifteen straight days when air quality in cities such as Fairbanks was deemed to be hazardous to health by Environmental Protection Agency standards.

In contrast, the 2007 fire season in Alaska was relatively unexceptional save for one notable event, the Anaktuvuk River tundra fire that accounted for nearly 40 percent of the acreage burned that year. Biologist Ben Abbott remembers it well. He and some colleagues were at the Toolik Field Station in northern Alaska playing a buggy game of soccer on a gravel pad when he smelled smoke.

Initially, Abbott thought nothing of it because smoke from fires in forests farther south in Alaska occasionally drifted into this part of the world. He and his colleagues quickly realized, however, that this smoke was coming from the north slope of Alaska, where there are no trees.

Tundra fires are relatively rare in the Arctic, and big tundra fires like this one had never happened in modern times. This fire had been ignited by a strike of lightning that had smoldered for a few months before strong, dry winds blowing in from the Brooks Range fanned the flames. More than 400 square miles of tundra burned before the October snowfalls finally put it out. The fire released as much carbon into the atmosphere as the tundra it burned had stored in the previous half century.

As unusual as this fire was, many scientists believe that it's only a matter of time before it will happen again. They are convinced that we have already entered a new fire regime that is more extreme than anything experienced in the boreal forest and tundra in the last ten thousand years, and they are not alone in thinking that. When the Canadian military traveled north in 2013 to conduct its annual exercises in the Arctic, it spent a good part of its time working with wildfire management teams on strategies for dealing with fires in the future. It was none too soon. The following year, the government of the Northwest Territories approached the military about the possibility of its personnel assisting in dealing with 295 fires that torched more than 7.5 million acres of forest in the Great Slave Lake area. The fires had so strained the resources of the territorial government that it had to borrow money.

These fires are intermittent but noticeable reminders of the Arctic's connection to the rest of the world. It is all too easy to go about our lives thinking of the vast region to the north, and what happens there, as a place of little consequence to our routines.

Vast, cold, remote, and unpopulated as the Arctic may be, what happens there matters to the rest of the world. Like El Niño, the warm ocean water temperatures that periodically develop off the Pacific coast of South America, a warming Arctic Ocean will likely trigger droughts, floods, and changes in crops yields in other parts of the world. It will further contribute to rising sea levels that are already imperiling low-lying coastlines along the Gulf of Mexico and other places. It has the potential to affect the polar jet stream that drives and gives energy to weather systems as it circles the world. It will also pollute the air we breathe down south. According to a study done by Gabriele Pfister and other researchers at the National Center for Atmospheric Research in Boulder, Colorado, the Alaska fires of 2004 produced 2.2 billion pounds of carbon monoxide, which is about the same amount produced by human-generated activities in the contiguous United States during the same period. Pollutants from these fires also increased ground-level ozone up to 25 percent in the northern continental United States and by up to 10 percent in Europe.

The changes already occurring in the Arctic are signs of what's to come in other parts of the world. With sea ice melting, glaciers receding, permafrost thawing, and Arctic storms picking up steam, dozens of low-lying coastal communities that are vulnerable to flooding and erosion, such as Shishmaref, Alaska, and Tuktoyaktuk, Northwest Territories, will have to be shored up or moved. A warmer and shorter ice season will result in less time for some polar bears to hunt seals and more time for mosquitoes and flies to take their toll on caribou. Increasingly powerful storm surges could result in massive seawater intrusions that could affect the fate of millions of migrating birds that nest in freshwater Arctic deltas and coastal wetlands. In addition, if freshwater from river runoff, melting sea ice, and disappearing glaciers continues to grow, the effects on climate and marine life in the Arctic could be enormous.

We can already see the rippling effects of some of these changes throughout the ecosystem. Capelin, not arctic cod, is the dominant fish in Hudson Bay; killer whales are beginning to prey on narwhals and beluga whales throughout the Arctic Ocean; Pacific salmon of all types are moving into many parts of the Canadian Arctic where they have never been seen before; and polar bears at the southern end of their range are getting thinner and producing fewer cubs than in the past (Figure 0.1). And with almost no ice left in the Chukchi Sea in late summer and fall these days, tens of thousands of walruses are now being forced to haul out onshore where they are farther afield from the clams, snails, and worms they eat and vulnerable to fatal stampedes that can occur when they get spooked. The haul-out of 35,000 animals off the coast of Alaska in late September 2014 was so dramatic that the Federal Aviation Authority took the unprecedented step of

Figure o.1 Along the west coast of Hudson Bay, polar bears are producing fewer cubs, and fewer are surviving beyond the first year of life than in years past. Photo credit: Edward Struzik

asking pilots to remain above 2,000 feet and half a mile away from the area, so as not to frighten the animals. Local community leaders also asked the media and other interested parties to stay away.

The changes are circumpolar in scope. In the Norwegian archipelago of Svalbard, fiords on the west coast have not been frozen for several years. Tundra there is being overtaken by shrubs, just as it is in Siberia and Chukotka in Arctic Russia. Like most glaciers in North America, the Greenland Ice Cap is melting faster than anyone had anticipated five or even two years ago.

There is actually very little we can do to stop the Arctic from warming in the short term. So much greenhouse gas is being emitted now that it would take decades if not centuries to halt or reverse the decline of sea ice cover, the thawing of the permafrost, the meltdown of the glaciers, and the acidification of the Arctic Ocean, all of which are directly attributable to the increase in carbon emissions. That's no reason not to try to curb these greenhouse gas emissions, however, and it's imperative that it be done.

Like the forest fire situation in 1950, however, there is merit in, as well as a powerful economic argument to be made for, using scientific knowledge and traditional aboriginal knowledge to manage the end of the Arctic world as we know it so that the new Arctic that is unfolding doesn't bring with it surprises that we aren't prepared to deal with or exploit. That's the message in a 2014 National Research Council report that attempted to look ahead to what awaits us as a new geological era unfolds. The committee members who wrote the report didn't do so independently. They called on hydrologists, mappers, oceanographers, biologists, weather analysts, sociologists, anthropologists, geologists, and others for their expertise and opinions.

The kinds of ecosystems that the new Arctic (including the sub-Arctic) will comprise, however, is not entirely clear because biodiversity in the region is not as simple as it is often made out to be. Against a backdrop of boreal forest, tundra, permafrost, polar deserts, glaciers, ice caps, mountains, rivers, deltas, sea ice, polynyas, gyres, and open ocean there are tens of thousands of pieces to this puzzle. They include the 21,000 cold-climate mammals, birds, fish, invertebrates, plants, and fungi that we know a lot about as well as the untold number of microbes and endoparasites that remain largely a mystery.

What we do know with some degree of certainty is that temperatures will rise dramatically in summer, resulting in the Arctic Ocean being seasonally ice-free by 2040. Two-thirds of the world's polar bears will be gone a decade later, as will one-third of the 45,000 lakes in the Mackenzie, the largest delta in the Arctic. In 2100, when trees and shrubs overtake much of the grasses and sedges on the tundra, what we think of as traditional habitat for barren ground caribou will have shrunk by as much as 89 percent. Coniferous forests will be replaced by deciduous ones in many places. Some trees will have begun to take root on the south end of the Arctic Archipelago. The polar ice cap on Melville Island will have melted away. Brintnell Glacier, the last remaining ice field on the mainland of the Northwest Territories, will be gone as well.

What we think we know about a future Arctic, however, may be grossly underestimated. By nature, scientists are slaves to certainty. If that certainty is 95 percent, as it is in scientists' belief that humans are responsible for the warming that has been taking place since 1950, there's confidence in telling the public.

Most scientists actually have a picture of a future Arctic that is much more daunting than the one they are comfortable talking about or putting pen to. Glaciologist Jason Box said as much when a writer for *Rolling Stone* asked him if high-end projections of a 6-foot rise in sea levels due to the meltdown of the Greenland Ice Cap are too low. "Shit yeah," said Box, who believes that dust and soot from forest and tundra fires and coal-fired plants from around the world are settling into the country's interior and absorbing more solar energy than most people think.

The only thing unique about Box is that he said out loud what many scientists think privately. When Ben Abbott and University of Florida researcher Edward Schuur asked forty-one climate experts what percentage of the surface permafrost is likely to thaw, how much carbon will be released, and how much of that carbon will be methane, the scientists surveyed predicted that the amount of carbon released by 2100 will be 1.7 to 5.2 times larger than reported in recent modeling studies, which used a similar warming scenario. The carbon released will be similar in scope to the carbon that is currently released by deforestation.

Abbott and Schuur also surveyed climate and fire experts in 2013, asking them how much boreal forest and tundra will burn in the future. Nearly all respondents painted a picture that is much worse than what most experts had publicly claimed. In a "business-as-usual" scenario, they predict that emissions from boreal forest fires will increase by 30 to 90 percent by 2040. In a "best-case" scenario, fire emissions will increase by 16 to 43 percent. Emissions from tundra fires will grow even more rapidly, in large part because they have been so rare in the past. In the same business-as-usual scenario, these scientists expect an increase in emissions that ranges from threefold to seventeenfold by 2100.

Fire scientist Mike Flannigan plants himself somewhere in the middle of the pack of these forecasters, but even he believes that we could see a Chinchaga-sized fire in the sub-Arctic sooner rather than later. If there has already been a fire in the boreal forest that spread into the Arctic tundra, he says, a fire of 1 million to 2 million hectares is not out of the question.

As much as we do know about what the future Arctic might look like, it's what we don't know that worries scientists like Henry Huntington, cochair of the National Research Council committee that examined emerging research questions in the Arctic. "Many of the questions we've been asking are ones we've been asking for some time," says Huntington, an Arctic scientist at the Pew Charitable Trusts, "but more and more, there are new questions arising from insights that have been made only in recent years, or phenomena that have only begun to occur."

The list of emerging questions is long, and they come from a number of unexpected developments. Consider, for instance, the following: the discovery that beluga whales and narwhals in the Arctic have little or no immunity to diseases such as phocine distemper that are common in midlatitude marine environments; the enormous irruptions of snowy owls in southern Canada, the United States, and as far south as the Caribbean in 2011 and 2013 that suggest that something might be happening to prey cycles in the Arctic; the storm surge of 1999 in the Mackenzie delta in Arctic Canada that sent a huge wave of seawater more than 20 kilometers inland, turning much of the tundra that was swamped into a dead zone; and the ridiculously powerful cyclone that tore through the Arctic for two weeks in the summer of 2012.

Underscoring that there is still a great deal to learn is the 2009 discovery of a flat-topped mountain ridge 3,772 feet above the seafloor 700 miles north of Alaska and 300 miles west of Ellesmere Island. Nearly 25 miles long and 12 miles wide, it is nothing short of remarkable that such an enormous geological formation could remain undiscovered for so long.

What the future holds for the Inuit, the Dene and Athabaskans, and other northern indigenous people whose cultures grew out of a close association with this frigid world is another part of the puzzle that needs to be put together. Those cultures are already in a state of rapid economic reorganization and social readjustment. Many people have either stopped or reduced their consumption of caribou and reindeer, not because they prefer store-bought beef and pork, but because the caribou and reindeer populations are collapsing all across the Arctic world.

Industrial changes that have come to the Arctic are bound to further destabilize this fragile world. No longer a wasteland of interest only to missionaries, miners, and outdoor adventurers, the Arctic now matters more than ever before. The receding ice is revealing 22 percent of the undiscovered, technically recoverable hydrocarbon resources in the world, and it is opening up shipping lanes that are far shorter, cheaper, and potentially safer than existing routes that must pass through the Panama and Suez Canals.

Exploited responsibly, the extraction of these resources could be a boon to a world economy increasingly starved of new sources of fossil fuels and metals. The development and exploitation of these resources could also solve some of the formidable economic and social problems that are impoverishing the Arctic's many indigenous communities.

Coming, however, at a time when Arctic animals such as the narwhal, beluga whale, and polar bear may be having difficulty adapting to these rapidly changing conditions, there are likely to be extinctions, extirpations, and trade-offs. Inevitably, sea ice will continue to be a problem, even if it thins to levels that make navigation through the Arctic safer. Accidents will happen, as the *Exxon Valdez* off the coast of Alaska proved. Oversights will fail, as British Petroleum's oil spill in the Gulf of Mexico demonstrated. Currently, there is no proven method by which cleanup crews can separate oil that is attached to ice, nor is there any infrastructure in place in the Arctic from which to stage a cleanup. An oil spill in the High Arctic could well be more catastrophic than anything we've seen so far.

The future is not entirely bleak. Arctic animals such as the musk ox will likely thrive in this warmer world. So, too, may the wood bison, which emerged from the nineteenth century greatly diminished due to habitat loss and overhunting before it was reintroduced to parts of the Northwest Territories, the Yukon, Siberia, and Alaska. There are even signs, which currently seem like long shots, that lions—the cougar in this case—could stage a comeback in a land in which it once preyed on animals such as the Yukon horse and the woolly mammoth. In addition, as Syndonia Bret-Harte, an ecosystem ecologist at the University of Alaska Fairbanks Institute of Arctic Biology, recently discovered, vegetation can recover from tundra fires as long as the fires are spaced far enough apart in time.

It would not be an exaggeration to suggest that the world is watching these developments unfold with great interest. The United States, Russia, Canada, Norway, and Denmark—all members of the Arctic Council that loosely oversees the exploitation and conservation of a changing landscape in the polar world—are currently in a race to claim millions of square miles of Arctic that belong to no one. In 2013, after years of trying to join, China, Japan, South Korea, Singapore, India, and Italy were finally granted observer status on the Arctic Council.

This newfound interest in an Arctic that is no longer as frozen, inaccessible, and seemingly worthless as it once was perceived to be will inevitably bring with it a different and more complicated set of beliefs in what this area is and what it means to the rest of the world. Therein lie questions that need to be answered before it is too late, although "too late" is difficult to define. In places like northern Alberta, development of the oil sands has already proceeded with little consideration for wetlands, wildlife, and the native peoples who live there.

What is the future of the Arctic, which is so intimately tied to the future of the more habitable places where we humans have settled in such great numbers? If there is anything that can be done to shape it so that economic and geopolitical interests don't sacrifice environmental and cultural integrity, which will no doubt have global reverberations, what will it be?

This book is an attempt to explore these questions in the midst of our scientific, cultural, and political uncertainties. The end of the Arctic that has existed for all modern time is upon us today. What it will look like in the future depends in part on the policies we choose to help shape what we—peoples from the south and peoples of the north—would like it to be.

Chapter 1

Eight-Foot-Long Beavers, Scimitar Cats, and Woolly Mammoths

What the Past Tells Us about the Future Arctic

A T BALLAST BROOK, on the north end of Banks Island in the Canadian Arctic Archipelago, the trunk of a spruce tree emerges from the eroding permafrost. Although it looks as if this tree might have died only two or three years ago, it has been entombed in an icy grave of peat and gravel for the past three million to five million years. This tree is a remnant of a boreal forest that once covered this stark tundra landscape.

In the summer of 1967, geologist Len Hills was hiking along this plateau at Ballast Brook when he spotted a large, fossilized bone protruding from the surface not far from that tree. It was cold, wet, and snowing at the time. Hills picked up the specimen, put it in his bag, and carried on without really knowing what he had found that day. Being a palynologist, he was more interested in finding the spores and pollen from the ancient plants that once grew here than what might have walked on four legs.

Hills didn't give the discovery another thought until Dale Russell, a paleontologist with the Canadian Museum of Nature, telephoned him some ten years later and asked whether he had ever come across some Cretaceous-era bones during his explorations in the High Arctic.

Hills thought it an odd request. At the time, very few scientists seriously considered the possibility that *Tyrannosaurus rex* and other dinosaurs had ever ventured anywhere near the polar world. It had never occurred to him that one or more of the unidentified fossils he had picked up during his many research expeditions to the Arctic could be that of a "terrible lizard."

Back in his lab, Hills searched for, and found, the fossil he had picked up at Ballast Brook that day. He gave it a wash and then had a good laugh when he and his colleagues finally figured out what it was. The fossil was not that of a dinosaur; rather, it was the shinbone of a woolly mammoth, a giant elephant-like animal that once lived in the Arctic.

For some time, no one knew what to make of that specimen or another mammoth fossil that was found on Melville Island to the northeast. Paleontologists knew that these big, hairy, elephant-like animals had lived in the Arctic at one time, but no one thought that their range extended beyond the north coast of the Yukon and Alaska on to the Arctic islands.

In time, paleontologist Richard Harington, the man who dated the fossil bone, came up with an explanation that seemed to satisfy most everyone then. Harington, arguably the world's most respected Ice Age paleontologist, suggested that Banks Island and parts of southwestern Melville Island were once part of the northeastern limit of Beringia, a verdant mass of lowland that periodically connected Arctic Russia to Arctic North America when sea levels were much lower than they are today because most of Earth's water was locked up in glaciers.

Over a period of tens of thousands of years, Harington suggested, most of those woolly mammoths that migrated across this continent-sized lowland would have slowly moved southeast into Canada until massive sheets of ice that periodically expanded northwestward from the Hudson Bay region stopped them. He thought that some of them, however, may have stayed behind or retreated north across the ice sheets that connected the mainland to Banks Island when sea levels were so low.

Even today, many scientists assume that much of Banks Island and other parts of the western Arctic Archipelago were largely ice-free through the last period of glaciation and at least partially ice-free for hundreds of thousands of years before that. You can almost see it in the soft, verdant look of this treeless tundra on a warmish summer day. In places such as the Thomsen River valley, the sedge- and grass-covered terrain looks as if it had never been scoured by the sharp edges and heavy weight of ice that expanded to its Ice Age maximum 18,000 years ago before petering out 7,000 years later.

For most of his forty-year career conducting research in the Arctic, scientist John England also thought that Banks Island was a relatively undisturbed relic of an ancient world. Sometime in the 1990s, however, he and a handful of colleagues in the paleoenvironmental community saw something in the accumulation of geological evidence that suggested that this theory might be flawed.

England and I were standing on the tundra at Ballast Brook, the site of Hills's mammoth bone find, in the summer of 2012 when he described to me how he saw it all unfold. It was cold and bleak that day in August, just as it might have been when Hills had been there more than four decades earlier. England was waving his arms, much like a sketch artist might do in a courtroom, drawing a picture of a monstrous sheet of ice moving north from the mainland in superslow motion, churning up granite and gravel, sand and stone, and possibly the bones of animals that may have died in its path (Figure 1.1). Banks Island may have been home to woolly mammoths and other Ice Age animals at one point in time, he told me, but if it had been, the animals were eventually displaced by this big sheet of ice.

"If there was such a population, it is surprising that no additional evidence has been found of any other animals like it," he said. "One bone on Melville, one on Banks? And the Melville sample was found below marine limit, the height of the postglacial sea level that inundated the land after ice retreat." He offered a different interpretation of the evidence: "That mammoth bone could have been rafted in by sea ice long after the animal from which it was derived, lived," he added. "How far away is anyone's guess."

England didn't arrive at this theory lightly.

The truth about how Banks Island and other parts of the Arctic have been shaped by climate, glaciers, and ice sheets has been germinating, evolving, and constantly changing as a result of the research that he, Harington, and many other scientists have been conducting

Figure 1.1 Canadian scientist John England stands by a tree trunk at Ballast Brook on the northwest coast of Banks Island where trees such as redwood grew as high as 22 meters and were as thick as 60 millimeters in diameter between 2 million and 10 million years ago. Photo credit: Edward Struzik

in the circumpolar world. It all it points to a region that has undergone massive changes over the eons.

For the longest time, putting together the pieces of the puzzle to get a picture of the past proved to be elusive because radiocarbon dating is generally not reliable for dating anything more than 50,000 years old. Additionally, many important pieces of the puzzle were buried in permafrost, snowpack, and riverbeds in the most inaccessible parts of the world. Those that were found offered only a snapshot, not necessarily strong evidence of the land's complex evolution.

No one in Hills's day, however, expected this once very blurry picture of the past to unfold as clearly as it has. Two Smithsonian scientists, Charles Schuchert and David White, returned from Greenland in 1897 bearing fossils that suggested that the Arctic wasn't always covered in snow and ice and that it was once a tropical paradise forested by giant sequoia–like trees rising up from an undergrowth of luxuriant ferns, tangled vines, and flowerless plants. Foremost among the discoveries that have transformed our understanding of the Arctic as a warm climate since then is Mary Dawson and Robert West's excavation of a rich vein of varied life-forms at Strathcona Fiord on Ellesmere Island in 1970s. In among the rocks, gravel, and peat they dug and sifted through, these American scientists found fossil fragments of alligators, giant tortoises, snakes, lizards, tapirs, hippos, and rhino-like animals that lived 55 million years ago in a climate that was similar to what is experienced today in Georgia and the Florida Everglades.

Equally important were the tree trunks that helicopter pilot Paul Tudge saw sticking out of the ground on Axel Heiberg Island in the High Arctic in 1985. The trees turned out to be more than 10 million years younger than the creatures Dawson and West had unearthed. Some of the dawn redwoods that paleobotanists James Basinger and Jane Francis later found were more than 16 feet long and 8 feet wide. The various nuts, seeds, and cones they collected were so perfectly preserved that they looked as if they had recently fallen to the ground. Several specimens still held the sap they oozed before a catastrophic flood buried and preserved them in an anaerobic tomb of sand. A single tooth found by paleontologists Jaelyn Eberle and John Storer some time later indicated that here was a world that was lush enough to sustain brontotheres, a rhino-like animal that was found in large numbers across Asia and North America.

In the years that followed, a picture of an enduringly warm Arctic came into sharper focus. Brontotheres, we now know, continued to thrive in a mixed conifer forest on and around Devon Island, located to the west of Baffin Bay from Greenland's coast, for several more million years. Four and a half million years ago, miniature beavers and three-toed horses lived in an upland environment at Strathcona Fiord where they were constantly on the lookout for ancestral bears, weasel-like carnivores, and Eurasian badgers that lurked in the adjoining forests 4.5 million years ago. And thanks to a recent discovery by Natalia Rybczynski, we also know that camels lived in the same region in larch-dominated wetlands a million years later.

As warm and verdant as the Arctic was for most of the past 100 million years, a trend to cooling began to take place shortly after smaller mammals replaced the dinosaurs 65 million years ago. The gradual buildup of glaciers and ice sheets that followed 20 million years later signaled the beginning of the end of the brontotheres. By the time miniature beavers had staked their claim at the north end of Ellesmere Island, a vicious cycling of advancing and retreating glaciers had begun to take hold, killing off vast swaths of forests throughout the Arctic Archipelago and northern mainland, including those that grew out of the ground at Ballast Brook.

I had trouble picturing this scenario until I spent several weeks with Jim Basinger at Axel Heiberg and then with Dick Harington at Strathcona Fiord, excavating fossils from stark hillsides of frozen peat and gravel. In both places, it seemed as though the summer was never going to come. The surrounding mountainsides were dusted with a fresh veil of snow, and a wickedly cold wind periodically swept snow squalls and sleet across sea ice that showed no sign of melting. Sifting through the peat on a high hilltop one day with Harington, I picked out a twig that had the bite of a beaver on its tip. Harington took it in hand, looked at it, and then pointed to the glaciers in the distance.

Starting sometime around 2.6 million years ago, he explained, summers could no longer melt the ice and snow that winters produced, and glaciers continued to grow in volume. Weighed down by the mounting snow, these rivers of ice began to slowly slide forward down mountainsides before plowing through forests and fanning across open plains.

So much of the world's water was locked up in ice and snow during most of this so-called Ice Age that sea levels dropped to levels that were up to 400 feet lower than they are today. In time, the shallow submarine world that connected Arctic Russia to Arctic North America was revealed. Attracted to the succulent grasses that rose up from these verdant lowlands, Asian animals like the mammoth,[1] saiga antelope, and steppe bison eventually crossed over to new lands, where they were met by scimitar cats, short-faced bears, and other North American predators.

On one hand, this enormous land bridge functioned as a gateway to new ranges for terrestrial animals, but on the other hand, it was a barrier that blocked whales, walrus, seals, and other marine mammals from migrating back and forth between the Arctic and North Pacific Oceans. The presence of this continent-sized land mass also put an end to the relatively warm freshwater that poured heat and nutrients from the North Pacific into the Arctic Ocean. The Arctic not only got colder, it got drier because so little moisture rose up from what little open water there may have been at the time. Additionally, the mounting sheets of ice reflected the heat of the sun back into the atmosphere.

As cold as it was for most of the past 2.6 million years, there were brief periods of intense warming. During these interludes, giant ground sloths migrated north to the Arctic from South America as did camels, pigs (peccaries), horses, American mastodons, and beavers the size of grizzly bears that lived farther north.

When the warming ended and the ice sheets returned, some of these animals found refuge in places such as the Old Crow Flats of the Yukon that were too dry and cold to grow ice. In time, though, most of the animals were unable to withstand the rapid-fire cycles of cooling and warming that followed. Among the thirteen species of mammals that Harington unearthed at Gold Run Creek in the west-central part of the Yukon Territory in the 1970s, seven of them—the giant short-faced bear, American Beringian lion,[2] American mastodon, woolly mammoth, horse, helmeted musk ox, steppe bison—are extinct. Two others, the American badger and the black-footed ferret, are no longer found in the Arctic.

What we have today are the survivors: a mere 11 Arctic bird species, 357 types of vascular plants, 12 terrestrial mammals, 3 Arctic whales, and a handful of other marine mammals that have found a way to live in the Arctic year-round.

If the past tells us anything about the future, it's that the current migration of deer, cougar, coyote, killer whales, and Pacific salmon into the Arctic is nothing new. Nor is the apparent decline of Arctic animals such as the polar bear, ivory gull, and caribou.

Taking this long view, Yukon paleontologist Grant Zazula believes there is much we can learn from this picture of the past that has been emerging. But he also believes that extinctions, local extirpations, and the like create opportunities for evolution. "Extinction," he argues, "is essential for evolution to be possible. Environmental change works like that too. It might be detrimental to one critter, like warming climates and forest expansion was for woolly mammoths, but it created a great opportunity for giant ground sloths to multiply and expand."

Zazula suggests that we should be careful in predicting who the winners and losers will be over the next 100 years. Many scientists, he points out, think that caribou will be hit hardest by climate-induced landscape changes that are expected to wipe out as much as 89 percent of their habitat. But if the history of caribou tells us anything, he says, it's that caribou managed to find refugia in the Arctic through several periods of glaciation over the past 1.6 million years. The same, he says, can be said about bison, which hung on until 400 years ago when something—no one knows what exactly—wiped out the last of them in the Yukon and Alaska.

Even the woolly mammoth almost made it. Scientist Duane Froese, working with Zazula, geneticist James Haile, and other scientists from Australia, Scotland, England, and the United States, recently found evidence along the Yukon River in Alaska that suggests that the woolly mammoth lived several thousand years longer than previously thought in so-called ghost ranges of the western Arctic.

It wasn't just climate and changing landscapes that killed off the last of the woolly mammoths. Theoretically, humans who crossed the Beringian land bridge 15,000 years or more ago contributed to demise of the woolly mammoth. The prospect of human influence on mammoth populations was nicely articulated in 2011 by palaeoecologist Glen MacDonald and his colleagues at the University of California, Los Angeles after they analyzed radiocarbon dates for mammoth specimens, archeological sites, and prehistoric plants and trees. Mammoth populations, they concluded, didn't go out with a big bang as some had previously thought. Instead, their numbers gradually declined as the Ice Age gave way to a warmer, wetter climate that transformed steppe lands into peat bogs, shrublands, and conifer forests. As the populations shrank into areas that were still covered by grasses and sedges, hunting by both humans and predators took its toll. Slow breeders that they were, the mammoths didn't have the reproductive ability to get out of this predator pit they were in.

The take-home message, says Zazula, who published a wider ranging paper on the subject with a long list of like-minded scientists, including lead author Eline D. Lorenzen, is that each species responds differently to the effects of climatic shifts, habitat redistribution, and human encroachment. Using ancient DNA, species distribution models, and the human fossil record, they concluded that climate change could in itself explain the extinction of some species, such as Eurasian musk ox and woolly rhinoceros, but it appears that a combination of climatic and anthropogenic effects is responsible for the extinction of others, including Eurasian steppe bison and wild horse. Interestingly, they found no genetic signature or any distinctive range dynamics that distinguished extinct from surviving species.

The big difference between now and then is that there are a lot more people living in or working in the Arctic. And they are not just hunting with spears and bows as they did when the first people ventured into the Arctic world at Yana River in Siberia 35,000 years ago. The prehistoric technology that they brought with them when they made their way across Asia, into Beringia, and then to the Arctic Islands pales in comparison to what people in the North use today. Even then, it seems, they may have helped drive some Ice Age mammal populations that had been pushed to the edge by climate change to extinction. What we consider to be normal wasn't part of the past history of the Arctic.

Today as well, humans are building roads to mine sites, drilling for oil and gas on land and offshore, shipping resources in and out of the region, setting up military bases, and growing their populations in places that may provide refuges for caribou and other Arctic animals that might have trouble adapting to changing land and seascapes.

The warming taking place in the Arctic is also accelerating faster than anything that has been documented over the past 2.6 million years. Those trees, shrubs, and peatlands that drove woolly mammoth and other Ice Age animals into smaller and smaller pockets of grasslands are once again migrating north, bringing with them the threat of fire that was once relatively low in the Arctic. And sea ice, which once prevented marine mammals like the killer whale from venturing north in pursuit of beluga whales and narwhal, is melting away.

Understanding effects of past environmental change, and their implications for current times, is only part of what is needed to get a sense of what current conditions of the Arctic might hold, however. The Arctic has a cultural and political history that bears heavily on how policy makers view the region, and past events indicate that they have not always used history and science well to inform prudent decision making.

Today's decision makers would do well to note the centuries of folly that have been a hallmark of nonaboriginal interactions in the Arctic.

The search for a northwest or northern passage to the Orient is a case in point. From the time Italian explorer John Cabot first set sail from Bristol, England, in 1497 in the small bark *Matthew* with a northwest or northern passage in mind to the moment almost 350 years later when all 129 crew members of John Franklin's expedition disappeared, more than 140 ships from Italy, Portugal, Britain, and the United States tried and failed to find an Arctic shortcut to the Orient. Not until Norwegian Roald Amundsen's small square-sterned sloop *Gjoa* sailed into Lancaster Sound and Barrow Strait in 1903 and rounded Point Barrow in Alaska three years later was the Northwest Passage successfully navigated.

The most enduring of the beliefs that drove these monumentally flawed and fabulously expensive efforts to find a shortcut to the Orient was one in an open polar sea at the North Pole. With few exceptions, Arctic explorers assumed that if they plowed far enough through the Arctic ice, they would reach a place where the effects of twenty-four hours of sunlight and other natural phenomena would be more than enough to make the region ice-free.

The idea of an open polar sea is a wonderful story. It has its origins in a Greek myth that describes open water beyond the Rhipean Mountains where Boreas, the purple-winged god of North Wind, lived in a land of eternal spring and twenty-four hours of daylight. Many people at the time thought it was Boreas's icy breath that brought winter to southern Europe.

Explorations to the edge of the Arctic by the Greek sailor Pytheas and by Venetian sailors Antonio and Nicolo Zeno appeared to lend credence to this concept of open water at the North Pole. Gerhard Mercator and Abraham Ortelius, two of Europe's most accomplished sixteenth-century cartographers, were so influenced by the Zeno map that was drawn in 1380, then lost, and found nearly 200 years later that they prominently displayed the Zenos' open polar sea on their own maps of the world.

No one knew at the time that the Zeno map was a hoax, an elaborate attempt, it seems, to debunk the notion that Christopher Columbus was the first to discover North America. To the day of his death in

1848, however, John Barrow, secretary to the British Admiralty and the main organizer of British polar exploration from 1818 to 1845, believed that the Arctic region harbored an open polar sea. So did American explorer Elisha Kent Kane, who sailed to the Arctic in 1853 to 1855. In his official report to the U.S. Navy, he included a map in which the words "Open Sea" are spelled out in bold letters over the North Pole.

When science, firsthand discovery, death, and tragedy finally led decision makers to concede that there was nothing beyond the ice pack in the Arctic but more ice, an image of the Arctic as a wasteland of interest only to missionaries, Royal Canadian Mounties, military strategists, and a handful of adventurers began to emerge.

Decision makers saw so little value in this icy real estate that they sold huge chunks of it off for a song. After a single night of wrangling in 1867, Russia turned over what is now the state of Alaska to the United States for $7.2 million, or about 2 cents per acre. A steal though this purchase has turned out to be, it was dubbed "Seward's Folly" at the time because critics believed that Secretary of State William H. Steward had bargained badly.

Russia wasn't alone in deeply discounting Arctic real estate. In 1930, Norway gave up its claim to the Sverdrup Islands in the Arctic Archipelago of North America for 13,767 pounds, 2 shillings, and 1 penny along with Great Britain's willingness to recognize Norwegian sovereignty over two islands along the northeast passage.

By 1949, the Arctic was regarded as being so worthless that a plan, labeled "top secret," was hatched to detonate twelve Hiroshima-sized atomic bombs along the west coast of Hudson Bay. Had this plan, officially called "The Technical Feasibility of Establishing an Atomic-Weapons Proving Ground in the Churchill Area," been approved, the bombs would have laid waste to a huge stretch of tundra in northern Canada. The blasts and the fallout would have also killed most of the one thousand polar bears that are forced to spend the summer and autumn on land waiting for cold weather to bring the ice back to the region.

The plan was the work of C. P. McNamara of Canada's Defense Research Board and William George (later Lord) Penney, the scientist who had participated in the Manhattan Project before moving on to direct Great Britain's Atomic Weapons Research Establishment.

They and other high-ranking decision makers decided on Churchill over several other similarly remote places in Canada because they considered it a "waste land suitable only for hunting and trapping." In a proposal that would have had the highest level of attention in the two governments, they reasoned that only the "occasional hunter or trapper" would be affected.

The Churchill plan, of course, was never approved. Instead, the winning proposal went to Australia, but only because the British believed that northern Canada would be too cold and uncomfortable for Australian scientists.

This image of the Arctic as a frigid wasteland of little value to anyone proved to be enduring even as scientific research began to paint a picture of a biologically productive world that harbored 5 million caribou and reindeer, 150,000 beluga whales, 80,000 narwhals, 100,000 musk oxen, 20,000 to 25,000 polar bears, and nesting grounds for millions of the world's birds.

No one in government seemed to care either that several distinct human cultures were tied to the movement of these birds and animals. Throughout the 1950s, the Soviet Union rounded up thousands of nomadic Arctic people and forcibly moved them to labor camps. Canada and Denmark did something similar. In 1953, the Danish government relocated the entire village of Thule in Greenland to a site 60 miles to the north to make room for a U.S. military base. That same year, the Canadian government shipped several families from northern Quebec 1,500 miles north to two virtually uninhabitable parts of the High Arctic as part of a plan to assert sovereignty in the region.

The pattern of decision making that emerged in those years continued for decades. Whenever sovereignty, security, and economic priorities came into play, environmental integrity and the cultural interests of indigenous northerners invariably suffered, as it did more recently when the *Exxon Valdez* spilled 11 million gallons of oil off the coast of Alaska in 1989.

Partially due to our mistakes in the past, we have now reached critical times for charting the course of the future Arctic. With rapidly melting sea ice resurrecting the image of an open polar sea, decision makers are once again looking at a shortcut through the Arctic and an economical way of shipping this frontier's oil, gas, and various mining minerals to southern markets. Canada, the United States, Russia, and Denmark are also frantically mapping vast, unclaimed regions of the Arctic in hopes of adding territory instead of selling it off or neglecting it as they once did. This territory, however, is often valued for its potential as an economic resource instead of for its environmental or ecological richness.

Realistically, there is no way we are going to stop sea ice and glaciers from melting away or trees and shrubs from taking over the tundra. Sea levels will rise, Arctic storms will pick up steam, and storm surges will extend their reach inland as each decade passes, but policy decisions can be made to mitigate the damage and to safely exploit the economic opportunities that will come as the Arctic's energy and mineral resources are revealed.

If the past tells us anything about the future Arctic, it's that climate change happens often, and when it does, it happens relatively quickly and sometimes catastrophically for mammals that lived there. With the climate warming up the polar world faster than any other place on Earth, the Arctic is some ways both an accident waiting to happen and an opportunity to be seized.

Notes

1. Technically, mammoths are Old World in origin. What is known as the "woolly mammoth" arose in North America sometime around 300,000 years ago and then spread into Asia. The first ancestral mammoths entered North America from Asia around 1 million years ago.

2. The lions of Yukon are now known to be part of the cave lions (*Panthera leo spelaea*) of Europe and Asia. The American lion (*Panthera leo atrox*) is genetically distinct, a result of isolation south of the North American ice sheets.

Chapter 2

Oil and Ice

WHEN AMERICAN ADVENTURER Walter Wilcox hiked up to Bow Summit in Banff National Park in 1896, he took a photo of a turquoise lake that caught the eye of a *National Geographic* editor some time later. In the photo that was eventually published in the magazine, the glacier feeding the lake was just 1 mile upstream, presumably still building, and slowly inching forward.

Since then, the snout of Peyto Glacier has receded more than 3 miles from the broad valley it carved out thousands of years ago. Remnants of ancient tree trunks that the glacier bulldozed during those colder times are now being spat out in the wake of its recent retreat. Even more striking is the effect of the glacier's dwindling flow of meltwater on the Mistaya and North Saskatchewan Rivers that it nourishes. Each year, Peyto is losing as much as 3.5 million cubic meters of water, roughly the amount that a city of 1.2 million people consumes in one day. With 70 percent of its ice mass already gone, Peyto is bleeding to death as a result of climate change that is melting snow and ice all over the world.

As unlikely as it may seem, clues to what a future Arctic will look like can be found here much farther south in the glaciers, snowpack, and massive ice fields that melt out of the eastern slopes of the Rockies.

This meltwater drains into dozens of small rivers like the Mistaya, the Whirlpool, and the Astoria before finding its way into the North Saskatchewan and South Saskatchewan Rivers, which drain into Hudson Bay, and into the Peace and Athabasca Rivers, which flow north into two of the world's largest deltas, the Peace-Athabasca and the Mackenzie, before spilling into the Beaufort Sea.

The Peace-Athabasca is one of the largest freshwater deltas in the world and unlike anything there is in the sub-Arctic. It is an ecological linchpin that stores massive amounts of water flowing to the Arctic for a remarkable array of fish and animals. In particular, it is a haven for the million tired birds that need a break on their long migration north and south along all four of North America's major flyways: the Atlantic, the Mississippi, the Central, and the Pacific.

In this 2,200-square-mile expanse of waterways and undisturbed wetlands that harbor abundance for both humans and wildlife, seasonally meandering rivers and streams can abruptly flow in opposite directions and flood their banks, especially when ice jams along narrow choke points. Big lakes and shallow streams can dry up one summer and reappear the next. Vulnerable as the delta is to climate change and to resource developments that are accelerating at a rapid pace upstream, it represents an accident waiting to happen.

For the Chipeywan, Cree, and Métis people who have lived in and around the delta for hundreds of years, the art of navigating through this landscape that was half land and half water was a lifelong lesson in recognizing these dangerous ebbs and flows. The rewards, however, were worth it.

Summers in the delta and on Lake Athabasca served up enough lake whitefish, lake trout, burbot, goldeye, walleye, pike, and various other fish to supply not only domestic needs, but also a commercial fishery. Autumn came with geese and ducks passing through to nest or stage for several days before continuing with the migration to the Mackenzie delta and other Arctic nesting grounds. In winter, there were plenty of moose and wood bison to hunt. By the time spring arrived, there were tern, gull, duck, and goose eggs to collect and enough muskrat to fill up a boat in a day. Muskrat and birds' eggs, in turn, supplied a steady source of food for mink, lynx, coyotes, and other predators.

Frank Russell, an American zoologist who spent five weeks in the delta in 1893 collecting waterfowl specimens, was impressed by what he saw there. As he described, "These channels swarm with muskrats and in the migratory season myriads of waterfowl halt upon the battures to feed, while a comparatively small number remain during the summer to breed in the adjoining marshes. More geese and ducks are killed there than at all other posts in the north. The big and little waveys (snow geese) are the most abundant and the most highly prized though swans and Canada geese, ducks and cranes abound."

The ecological importance of the Peace-Athabasca delta has not gone unnoticed by decision makers. In 1922, when Wood Buffalo National Park was established to protect the world's last three hundred free-roaming wood bison, 80 percent of the delta was included in the boundaries. In 1982, the delta was designated a United Nations World Heritage Site and a Ramsar Site of International Significance (Figure 2.1).

A half century ago, almost everyone living in and around the delta trapped and fished. Today, however, that percentage has dropped to the single digits. Cowboy Joe Wandering Spirit, a seventy-four-year-old Cree man who lives in a single-room cabin on the shores of the Quatre Fourche River, is the last person still living in the delta year-round. When I last saw him in 2010, his only company was a team of ten sled dogs and a crazy chewed-up cat that wouldn't let me get within 10 feet of Wandering Spirit.

As unfathomable as it might have once seemed, the delta is drying up. Heading into the spring of 2014, the flooding that is required to fill its shallow lakes had not occurred in any meaningful way since 1997. As a result, hundreds of those lakes have been drying up, and woody shrubs are overtaking vast areas of grass and sedge meadows.

The numbers tell the story. Following the flood of 1997, 55 percent of the north end of the delta where Joe lives was covered in water or shallow marshes. By 2008, that figure had fallen to 33 percent. The south end of the delta, which is recharged by the Athabasca River, is in better shape, but it, too, is steadily becoming drier.

I had first heard of the so-called death of the delta in the early 1980s when I spent two weeks visiting native peoples at their spring and summer camps. It was a tough trip for a greenhorn like me, more

Figure 2.1 The Peace-Athabasca is one of the world's largest inland freshwater deltas. Climate change and industrial and hydro developments upstream are contributing to its demise. Photo credit: Edward Struzik

comfortable in the St. Elias Mountains of the Yukon from my time in the national parks service than in the muskeg of the delta, bug-filled wetlands that overlay thick layers of dead plants in various states of decomposition. If it wasn't the mosquitoes tormenting me, it was the bulldogs, the giant biting horseflies that are relentless in their efforts to home in on the most tender and vulnerable parts of human flesh. One man I stayed with at his camp at Mamawi Lake didn't speak any English. Another trapper preferred not to talk much. Had I known then what I know now, I might have realized why.

The most memorable was an elderly Métis man named Frank Ladouceur. It was late in the evening when a fisherman dropped me off unannounced at Ladouceur's cabin at Big Point, on the Athabasca side of the delta. Ladouceur was sitting on the steps at the time playing jigs and country waltzes on his fiddle in between breaks to take a drag on his tobacco pipe. There was nothing much else for him to do. A massive spill from the Suncor oil sands plant upstream during the winter of 1982 had shut down the domestic and commercial fishery. The smell of petroleum still lingered in some of the fish that were being pulled out.

Ladouceur and I got off to an inauspicious start that first night, with me sleeping uncomfortably on the hard floor beside a partially covered pail of bear fat while he snored loudly on a bunk above me. Some time in the middle of the night, I woke up to the sight of him aiming a rifle, first at my head, then at the door behind me. I thought I was going to die when he fired a shot. "God damn bear," he yelled. "They steal vegetables from my garden and try to get what little I have inside. Now I have to skin that son-of-a-bitch and put a new screen on the door."

Ladouceur was the great-grandson of a Métis man who had lost his claim to land in Manitoba after the Riel Rebellion of 1875. Ladouceur's father eventually settled along the shores of the delta when Frank was just a year old. Preferring life on the trapline to a wooden desk in a single-room schoolhouse, Frank spent half the year in the bush alone when he was just a young teenager. It was, he told me, such a good life that he refused to give it up even when his wife had had enough and moved to town with the kids during the cold winter months.

It's not that he and other delta people like Cowboy Joe Wandering Spirit shunned the comforts of town. Fort Chipewyan was never more than a long day's ride away by boat, snowmobile, or dogsled. They would come in often to sell their fish and furs, resupply, celebrate, and visit with family. That's how Frank won the Northwest Territories fiddle championship one year. That's also how Cowboy Joe got his name. His Cree name used to be Dragonfly, but one night after celebrating a bit too much, he stole one of the town's water-drawing horses and took off with a cowboy hat on his head. It was several hours before the local Mounties finally got their man.

The good life, however, began to unravel in the late 1960s when water levels at the north end of the delta began dropping dramatically. Frank and his fellow trappers had seen water levels rise and fall before, but they had never seen anything quite as dramatic as this time. In some places on the Peace River side of the delta, it got so bad that some men were using their dog teams to pull their skiffs across Mamawi Lake. Andrew Campbell, an Orkney man who had married a Cree woman, watched in disbelief as water near his cabin at Egg Lake, one of the larger water bodies in the delta, dried up completely.

As water declined, so did muskrat, the nesting birds, and the quality of fish the men hauled in. "The delta was dying," Frank told me, "but none of us knew why. Some thought it was God taking revenge on us for being sinful. The old priest in town told us to pray for forgiveness. He blamed it on us for missing so many summer masses."

The problems of the Peace-Athabasca delta began in 1967 with completion of a 600-foot-high reservoir that was built to support a hydroelectric dam upstream along the Peace River in British Columbia. Designed to hold 47 million acre-feet of water, Williston Lake was, for a time, the eighth largest human-made reservoir in the world.

The Canadian government knew then that the dam would have an enormous effect on the delta downstream, but no one bothered to tell anyone who lived there.

Even after the reservoir was finally filled, the hydrology that drives the delta system never fully recovered. Initially, scientists suspected that a big part of the problem lay in the river flow regulation that was required to keep the turbines turning. To keep the flow steady, B.C. Hydro needed to hold back river water during the crucial winter and spring months when water volumes used to be sufficient to periodically create ice jams and flooding in the delta. Government scientists and engineers tried to mitigate the damage by building rock weirs and artificial ice dams along key choke points. It worked, but not as well as hoped. The weirs restored the natural summer peak water levels in the larger delta lakes but not the seasonal fluctuations that were critical in springtime.

Over time and after much more research, those same scientists realized that river flow regulation has not had a significant effect on the ice jams that cause the Peace to overflow its banks at various trigger points in the delta. The absence of flooding, it turns out, is linked more to diminishing snowpack in the upper tributaries of the river than to the way the water flow is regulated.

This situation can be seen in the floods that occurred in 1972, 1974, 1994, 1996, and 1997. In each case, there was a lot of snow in the mountains and boreal uplands and plenty of rain adding to the volumes of water flowing downstream.

What the future holds for the delta could be worse. Because the climate is warming, the mountains and boreal uplands downstream are not producing meltwater and groundwater the way they used to. An increasing percentage of the water that is produced is evaporating as a result of rising temperatures and the destruction of wetlands. Between 1970 and 2003, May to August streamflow along the Athabasca near Fort McMurray—the hub of oil sands extraction—declined by a little more than a third.

The rapidly melting glaciers and ice fields in the Rockies, which contribute about 8 percent of the water that flows into Lake Athabasca and the delta, are not going to make up for declines. From 1920 to 2005, three hundred of the glaciers there disappeared. In that same time, the area covered by glaciers declined by at least 25 percent.

In a way, the rapid retreat of glaciers is masking the effects of a much bigger water problem the delta will face in the future. In this respect, the situation may be worse than it seems. Neither the Peace nor the Athabasca River has yet felt the effects of snowpack declines and glacial retreats that are occurring on the more southerly Rocky Mountain rivers that drain northwest into Hudson Bay (Figure 2.2).

Snowpack and glacier-tracking scientists, however, know that the tap is going to begin to run dry eventually. Since 1890, the Athabasca Glacier, one of the six big icy toes that jut out of the massive Columbia ice fields, has lost half its volume. Each year, the toe of the glacier recedes by as much as 30 feet. The situation is even worse along the headwaters of the Peace River because the glaciers there are much smaller and more likely to disappear altogether by 2100.

"Climate change is not going to be kind to the glaciers of the Rockies," says Brian Menounos, who was part of a team that conducted a satellite inventory of glacial retreat that occurred in British Columbia and Alberta between 1985 and 2005. "By the turn of the century, most of the small glaciers will have disappeared," he adds.

Not only is this situation likely to contribute to a further drying of the delta, it could also result in water levels in Lake Athabasca dropping by more than 6.5 to 9.8 feet, one study predicts.

The future, of course, is speculative because it is based on a complex combination of wind, temperature, precipitation, snowpack, and glacier volumes. To some, the future of the delta looks more promising than to others. Scientist Stewart Rood and his colleagues have recently come up with data that suggest that the decline in the Athabasca that was documented in the past was part of a short-term pattern that may be associated with a phase transition of the Pacific Decadal

Figure 2.2 The Brintnell (shown here) is the last remaining ice field on the mainland of the Northwest Territories in Canada. Scientists expect it will disappear entirely by the end of the century as the climate heats up. Photo credit: Edward Struzik

Oscillation, an El Niño–like pattern of climate variability that occurs in the North Pacific. The declines in river flow, Rood says, did indeed occur. But if one extends the record back to a century in the Rockies, he says, one finds that the flows of 1970 to 2000 were unusually high.

Rood has no doubt that climate change is very real and that it is having a big effect on water that flows from the mountains into North and South Saskatchewan Rivers that flow into Hudson Bay. But he thinks that the boreal forest of northern Alberta may be entering the wet phase that one sees in climate models and that an increase in precipitation in the boreal forest could offset declines of snowpack at higher elevations.

If that is the case—and there are scientists who strongly disagree—it gives decision makers some time to reconsider their stance on how water flowing into the Athabasca delta and into Athabasca Lake will be affected by oil sands extraction and other upstream developments. One such project is Site C, a proposed large-scale earth-fill hydroelectric dam that would flood more than 12,000 acres of land in northern British Columbia.

As massive as it is, Site C's effect on the delta will likely be minor compared with the amount of water that the oil sands in Alberta is expected to divert from the Athabasca River in the future. It takes a tremendous amount of water to drive the oil sands industry. In 2010, the oil sands produced 1.6 billion barrels of crude every day. Net freshwater use in oil sands production in 2010 averaged about 3.1 barrels of water per barrel of oil produced by mining operations. So, for every barrel of oil, 2.6 barrels of water were withdrawn from the Athabasca River.

For in situ operations, where steam is used to separate the oil from the sand below and pump the bitumen to the surface, freshwater use averaged 0.4 barrel of freshwater per 1.0 barrel of oil. About a third of this water comes from groundwater aquifers, 44 percent from saline groundwater and 22 percent from surface water.

Oil sands operations return almost none of the water they use back to the natural cycle because the water is then toxic and therefore subject to a zero discharge policy. Wastewater that is not recycled is stored in tailings ponds. Wastewater from in situ processes is routinely reinjected into aquifers.

As things stand now, water diverted from current and approved oil sands operations amounts to 2.5 percent of the natural flow of the river. This figure could be as high as 10 percent in winter, when water volumes in the river are at their lowest. With oil sands production expected to triple by 2030, the amount of water being diverted from the Athabasca could be as high as 30 percent of its natural flow. Some energy industry economists are already suggesting that the oil sands could face water shortages by then.

We know that low water levels can be hard on or even lethal to spawning fish and the eggs they produce. A low water level not only starves them of oxygen, it concentrates pollutants that are naturally occurring or introduced to the river system.

Low oxygen levels on the Athabasca are now a fact of life in winter, as are high levels of polycyclic aromatic hydrocarbons (PAHs), which occur naturally in the Athabasca River and its tributaries. In high concentrations, PAHs are linked to embryonic deformities in fish.

For a long time, no one could say with scientific certainty whether an increase in oil sands mining has increased PAH concentration downstream of Fort McMurray because the baseline data that are needed to determine it have never been collected in any meaningful way. In 2013, however, an Environment Canada study demonstrated clearly that PAHs in six nearby lakes have risen roughly at the same pace as development along those lakes. Results in one remote lake showed PAH levels twenty-three times higher than predevelopment levels fifty years ago.

It's not altogether clear just how far this pollution is traveling downstream, but Environment Canada scientists recently discovered rising levels of mercury in the eggs of birds nesting in the delta. Eggs of ring-billed gulls collected from Mamawi Lake in 2012, for example, had 139 percent more mercury than they did in 2009. Smaller increases of mercury were also found in three species of gulls and terns at Egg Island.

It's possible, although unlikely, that the mercury is coming from some other source, but the petroleum industry is the largest source of mercury emissions in the province. What's more, mercury in eggs from California gulls nesting in the southern part of the province, far from oil sands development, declined by 57 percent between 2008 and 2012.

Unfortunately, water quality in the delta has been an issue since 1977 when a group of scientists conducting oil sands research warned the Canadian government that the effects on the environment downstream might be perilous and needed to be evaluated. Alberta's Environment Minister David Russell, however, very publicly dismissed their concerns and suggested that they "come down from their ivory towers, and concern themselves with relevant matters . . . that have a ready application for large scale oil sands development."

What followed were mounting environmental liabilities such as giant effluent ponds, denuded wetlands, and diminishing plant and wildlife populations. The Canadian and Alberta governments ignored it all until aboriginal people living downstream of the oil sands began exerting treaty rights and launching court challenges.

The breaking point for aboriginal people came in the winter of 1981–1982 when a series of fires and explosions at the Suncor oil sands plant resulted in massive amounts of oil, grease, and phenols spilling into the Athabasca River. People like Frank Ladouceur, Cowboy Joe Wandering Spirit, and Andrew Campbell were unaware of what had happened until a month later when several people in Fort MacKay, a small aboriginal community immediately downstream of Suncor, started complaining of nausea, headaches, and intestinal problems. Only then were they told of the fires and the breach of the tailings pond.

When the government of Alberta refused to take legal action against the company, Dorothy McDonald, chief of the Fort MacKay Indian band, filed her own charges under the federal Fisheries Act. It was a rare show of force from an aboriginal leader in northern Alberta at the time. Embarrassed by the public outcry, the government of Alberta took over the case, as was its legal right to do.

I was the only journalist from the south covering the Suncor trial in Fort McMurray, and it was clear to me that the government had no serious intention of securing a conviction. From the beginning, the young lawyer assigned to the case was in over his head against the expert legal team that Suncor had assembled. Day after day, I watched this lawyer peer down at a blank sheet of paper, unable to mount any kind of meaningful prosecution. Defense lawyers could barely contain their smiles. The judge was not amused and said as much on several occasions.

Then one day, the lawyer disappeared altogether without warning. Trying to figure out what why, I requested a conversation with the judge in his chambers. In a rare case of judicial disclosure, the judge informed me that Mounties had searched for hours before they had found the lawyer babbling in his hotel room. The Mounties, he said, were arranging to have him flown back to Edmonton.

In an effort to reassure the public that it was serious about pollution, the government hired a team of talented lawyers and expert witnesses to see the trial through. Suncor was finally brought to justice, but the $8,000 fine levied against the company after several weeks of damning testimony left Ladouceur and other people living in the delta still feeling like victims. To compensate for the losses that they had incurred as a result of the closure of the fishery, the government of Alberta gave sixty-two of them a total of $45,000 in hardship money. Some got as a little as $12 under the distribution scheme.

In the decades that followed, calls for better monitoring and oversight programs went unheeded until David Schindler, a world-renowned freshwater ecologist, almost single-handedly proved that the environmental monitoring system that had been put in place by

government and industry could not adequately track pollution downstream. It was what one journalist called a "David and Goliath" story,
with industry and government attacking Schindler at every opportunity before finally conceding that he was right.

Simply monitoring what is happening downstream is not enough
for people living in the delta. They know as well as anyone that industry's opportunity creates accidents that others have to suffer through.
Many of them fear that a spill like the one in the winter of 1981–1982
might recur. "Mark my words, it's going to happen, maybe not in my
lifetime because I'm seventy-four years old," Ray Ladouceur, Frank's
son, told me when I caught up with him in the spring of 2014. "When
it does happen, that will be the end of the delta."

Ray had good reason to believe that such a spill could happen. Just
a year earlier, the failure of a tailings pond at the Obed Mountain
coal mine in Alberta sent 670,000 cubic meters of mine waste gush-
ing down two creeks that drain into the Athabasca River. The waste
contained 90,000 metric tons of clay and coal sludge laden with arse-
nic, mercury, cadmium, lead, and manganese. The plume of pollutants
migrated several hundred kilometers downstream to Fort McMurray
before dissipating sufficiently to prevent harm to the delta. Even then,
detectable levels of contaminants were found there a year later.

The oil sands landscape, of course, is much closer to the delta than
the Obed mine site is. It is also a very different place now than it was in
1982 when there were only two companies mining for bitumen. Production has increased dramatically and so has the amount of toxic tailings.

These issues will have to be addressed responsibly if we want to
safeguard the delta and the waters that flow into the Arctic. Fifty percent of the water that flows into the Mackenzie River basin comes
from the Peace and Athabasca Rivers. Along the Athabasca, there are
now 1,000 trillion liters of tailings being stored in effluent ponds that
together cover an area close to 77 square miles. Some of these ponds
are more than 200 feet deep.

Ray Ladouceur is not alone in thinking that a spill from one of
these tailings ponds could happen. In 2012, the Rosenberg International Forum on Water Policy at the University of California issued a
report that suggested that the potential for a collapse or breach of one

of the tailings pond's dikes is a significant threat not only to the delta, but also to the entire Mackenzie River watershed downstream.

The distance between the oil sands and the Arctic Ocean is a long one, and virtually all of it passes through virgin country. From the Peace-Athabasca delta, water flows into the muddy Slave River, which drains into Great Slave Lake, one of the largest and cleanest lakes in Canada and one of the deepest lakes in the world. From the southwest corner of Great Slave, clear water flows into the Mackenzie before being clouded up by silty water that flows in from the Liard River.

Beyond the confluence of the Liard, the Mackenzie is big and slow moving, falling only 400 feet over 1,500 miles. In many places, it is 4 miles wide and up to about 25 feet deep. There are only two rapids, the San Sault, where the Mountain River joins, and the Ramparts, which are upstream of the small Sahtu community of Fort Good Hope.

Like the Peace-Athabasca delta, the Mackenzie is an extraordinary ecosystem. Not only is it the largest intact delta in North America, it is twelfth largest in the world. It is so big that the 235-square-mile Kendall Island Bird Sanctuary, summer home to sixty thousand nesting shore-birds, represents less than 5 percent of the area that the delta covers.

Before the Mackenzie River reaches the Arctic Ocean, it branches into three main channels. Ice jams along one or more of these channels cause them to overflow their banks just as it used to do in the Peace-Athabasca with some degree of regularity. That is how most of the forty thousand lakes in the Mackenzie delta are maintained.

Once the ice breaks up, it sends enormous pulses of relatively warm, nutrient-rich river water north. These so-called javes advance the melting of ice in both the delta and the nearshore ocean by several weeks. The biological importance of this surge of water is only beginning to be understood, but there is little doubt that it has a big effect on phytoplankton, algal growth, fish, and marine mammals, including the seven thousand beluga whales that spend a good part of the summer in the Mackenzie estuary. Oceanographers also believe that javes play a role in the way water circulates in the Arctic Ocean.

In the event of a massive breach of one of the oil sands tailings ponds, this downstream ecosystem would be extremely vulnerable. It would exacerbate changes in water chemistry that are caused by

permafrost thawing and slumping, forest fires accelerating, and precipitation patterns that are changing through the region.

Like the Cree, Chipewyan, and Métis who live in and around the
Peace-Athabasca delta, the Inuvialuit who live in and around the
Mackenzie delta are beginning to see changes. The mental maps they
have relied on to get from one body of water to another are becoming
a puzzling maze that no longer leads them so readily to the grizzly
bear, moose, muskrats, lynx, mink, and other wildlife that they hunt
and trap.

"River banks are slumping, channels are changing, and some lakes
are disappearing," Inuvialuit elder Danny Gordon said several years
ago when I kayaked the river on my own. "You don't find animals
where they used to be. The delta is not the same place it was twenty or
even ten years ago. It's changing, big time."

If Wilfrid Laurier University scientist Philip Marsh is right, the
changes Gordon is seeing are a harbinger of even bigger things to
come. Marsh and Lance Lesack of Simon Fraser University predict
that as many as a third of those forty thousand lakes in the delta could,
under certain conditions, dry up in the next thirty years.

Once again, climate is the biggest reason. Here and in other parts
of the western Arctic, temperatures are rising even faster than they
are in the Rocky Mountains and boreal forest to the south. Over the
past century, mean annual temperatures have, on average, risen 2 to 3
degrees Celsius, with the greatest increases occurring during the past
thirty years. The result is fewer ice jams and less of the flooding that is
needed to keep approximately a third of those lakes from drying out.

There is no doubt that some of the changes in the Mackenzie are
being triggered by natural processes that are always at play in a complex and poorly understood ecosystem like this one. Marsh, though,
believes that lower flood levels could, and probably will, add to the
losses that would normally occur.

The demise of both the Mackenzie and Peace-Athabasca deltas
would be catastrophic both for the people who live in the regions and
for the rich diversity of life that exists there. The Mackenzie basin is
arguably the largest undisturbed ecosystem in the world, a "cold Ama-
zon" some call it. Approximately 700,000 square miles of it is covered
by forest, most of it virgin. Nearly 20 percent of it is wetland and

tundra. There are 215 species of birds and 53 species of fish found here, including some fish with genetics that suggest that they originated in the Mississippi River and its tributaries. Pike and whitefish dominate the river system. There have, however, been recent signs that all six species of salmon are increasingly migrating upstream along the Mackenzie into Great Slave Lake and up the Slave River.

At last count, there were 400,000 people living in this watershed. The vast majority of them are non-native people living in places like Fort McMurray and Fort St. John upstream of the Peace-Athabasca. Most of the rest are Cree, Chipeywan, Métis, Dene, Gwich'in, and Inuvialuit who live farther north in remote regions.

Creating a road map to the future in this part of the world is not going be easy when three provinces, two territories, and the Canadian government are often at odds with one another over energy development, water conservation, and environmental protection. Cultural considerations are also problematic. The history of the Arctic is also one in which Inuit and First Nations interests have played second fiddle to economic, military, and sovereignty imperatives.

In addition to dramatic reductions in carbon emissions, needed are both a well-funded, robust monitoring program for the entire Mackenzie basin and legal institutional arrangements that allow for water to be managed holistically.

The Rosenberg Forum proposed such a program in 2012, but it bears repeating that there needs to be a master agreement that takes into account scientific and aboriginal knowledge. The way experts who contributed to the Rosenberg Forum see it, their program would be administered by a board of stakeholders who would have the financial wherewithal and some authority to decide how the watershed would be managed in the future. The board would be advised by an international scientific advisory committee whose members would have no vested interest in regional economic imperatives.

Industry also needs to start putting up bonds to pay for the environmental damage that might come from a major oil spill and pay for the water it uses and abuses. Giving water to the oil sands for free and allowing companies to reinject it back into the ground or into tailings ponds in a polluted state is a huge mistake, one that robs future generations of an increasingly threatened resource.

At some point along the way, demand for water along the Athabasca is going to hit a wall. In 2013, proposed and current projects had the capacity to withdraw more than 15 percent of the Athabasca River's water flow during its lowest flow periods. This demand for water is going to rise dramatically given that that oil sands production will increase from 2 million barrels per day in 2012 to 5 million barrels by 2030. By then, it's going to be too late to do anything meaningful about the environmental and cultural effects that this water withdrawal will have downstream.

As left of center as this idea of paying for water may sound, it recently got a nod of approval from Clement Bowman, a former vice president of Esso Petroleum and one-time research manager at oil sands giant Syncrude Canada. Using a systems methodology approach to investigate water quality and quality problems in Canada's oil sands, he and his colleagues evaluated five alternatives: (1) continuing with the status quo, (2) setting performance standards, (3) putting a price on water, (4) establishing tradable water rights, and (5) storing water for future use. The status quo is clearly the worst way to move forward because it does not encourage private companies to develop and employ new technologies related to water reduction. They concluded that water charges and trading rights are the best ways to ensure water security for the industry while balancing environmental and social effects.

There are models that point the way forward. In Texas, a state that shares Alberta's free-enterprise, no-holds-barred, pro-energy values, water that flows from the Edwards Aquifer is managed in a way that allows for both economic growth and conservation of plants and animals.

Located in north-central Texas, the Edwards Aquifer discharges about 900,000 acre-feet of groundwater annually, making it the most prolific artesian aquifer in the world. Depending on the aquifer for their water needs, however, are some two million people living in an area covering 4,350 square miles, including those who live in San Antonio, the seventh largest city in the United States.

For nearly a century, ranchers, farmers, industry, and municipalities engaged in costly court battles to determine who owns, who controls, and who can use the aquifer. Water was used and abused in almost every imaginable way. In the end, it was the fate of a handful of blind, colorless animals whose lives depend on the aquifer that resolved the issue. In 1991, the Lone Star Chapter of the Sierra Club filed a lawsuit against the U.S. Fish and Wildlife service claiming that the agency was failing to protect endangered species such as the Texas blind salamander, Comal Springs beetle, San Marcos gamusia, and several other aquatic and subterranean species that live in the aquifer and are found nowhere else in the world.

After a two-year trial, a federal court judge ruled in favor of the Sierra Club and other groups that eventually joined in the litigation. The judge ordered the Texas legislature to come up with a regulatory plan that would limit withdrawals from the aquifer, ensuring maintenance of adequate habitat for the species in question.

Seeing that they had little choice, except perhaps to turn ownership of the aquifer over to the federal government, state lawmakers replaced the Texas Underground Water District with the Edwards Aquifer Authority. The Authority is now responsible for the study, protection, and enhancement of the aquifer through the administration of research and regulatory programs. Doing so includes overseeing water quality regulations, monitoring the aquifer's recharge zone, maintaining water quality protection and response programs, overseeing well construction and well closings, supervising range management and conservation easement programs, developing and conducting hydrogeologic studies, and collecting basic hydrologic data.

The Authority is self-sustaining. It receives no money from the state. Funding comes from management and user fees, which include $47 per acre-foot authorized for municipal/industrial wells and $2 per acre-foot for pumped agricultural wells. By most accounts, the Authority's groundwater permit program serves as an effective tool in managing use of the region's primary water resource by limiting withdrawals from the Edwards Aquifer to 572,000 acre-feet per year, as required by the Edwards Aquifer Authority Act.

At one time, critics claimed that this approach would stymie economic growth, but that has proved not to be true. Even though the city of San Antonio has not increased water usage since 1996, its population has grown by more than 60 percent. Furthermore, city officials believe that under certain scenarios, there will be enough water for the additional 1.1 million people expected to live in the region by 2060.

What's even more remarkable is how comfortable Texans seem to be with this arrangement. When I visited San Antonio in the spring of 2013, the region was in the midst of a prolonged drought. Newspapers and television stations were awash with stories about the need to stop watering lawns, washing cars, and using too much water. The cab driver who drove me into town knew all about the aquifer and reminded me of the need to conserve. No one, it seemed, minded. In fact, I detected a sense of civic pride in the more than 110 miles of pipeline in San Antonio that deliver high-quality recycled water for use by golf courses, parks, commercial users, and industrial customers, as well as San Antonio's famous River Walk. If Texas can do such things, I wondered, why can't Alberta?

As gloomy as the future looks for the Mackenzie and the Peace-Athabasca deltas, there is still time to do something about it. I was reminded of that in May 2014 before embarking on a trip to the Canadian Rockies to have another look at how much farther the Peyto and the Athabasca Glaciers had retreated since I had last visited with glaciologists. Kevin Timoney, a former Parks Canada biologist who has written *The Peace-Athabasca Delta: Portrait of a Dynamic Ecosystem* about the natural history of the delta, informed me that delta had flooded significantly for the first time since 1997. Water, he said, was everywhere. The first thing that came to mind was that Stewart Rood may be right: perhaps the climate models showing the boreal forest of northern Alberta entering a "wet phase," with precipitation levels that could offset declines of snowpack at higher elevations, are correct.

There is, however, as Timoney says at the end of his book, another reason to be optimistic. The delta will never be mined, logged, or fragmented by energy developments because 80 percent of it is protected by a national park. Even without oil sands expansion or Site C development, however, the delta will be a vastly different place in the future just as it is different today than it was a century ago. The cold, hard fact is that Site C will be completed eventually, and despite heroic efforts from environmentalists, oil sands' expansion will proceed in the near term. The tensions of opportunity and inevitability of accidents hang in the balance with other changing elements of the Arctic environment.

Chapter 3

The Arctic Ocean

A Sleeping Giant Wakes Up

IN THE SUMMER OF 2012, I was in Bethune Inlet off the west coast of Devon Island in the eastern Arctic, searching for signs of a whaling ship that had spent nearly a year there 150 years ago. I should have also been watching out for icebergs and rocky shoals. Theoretically, inflatables like the one my companions and I were traveling in are designed not to sink, but shortly after a sharp rock sliced a hole in the bottom of the boat, the icy water began filling it up faster than we could bail it out with the boat's single bucket.

My instincts suggested that we get to shore as quickly as possible, but Valentine Ribadeau Dumas, the second mate and science officer on this Arctic sailing trip, had another plan. "Keep bailing," she shouted as she turned our "sinking ship" away from the shoreline and back toward our 47-foot yacht, which was now out of sight, anchored in safer waters more than a mile away. "The Zodiac is no good to us on land if it can't get us back to the boat," she explained. "It'll be a long time before anyone can come in and rescue us out there."

I realized that she was right. The barren, glacier-covered shoreline was clearly better suited to musk oxen and polar bears than to four humans without sufficient food, dry clothes, or shelter. So, I emptied the toolbox at my feet and started bailing as fast as I could, praying that the inflatable boat's finicky four-stroke engine wouldn't swamp and cut out as we continued to sink.

It was mid-August, and we were on the third leg of a five-week journey from Greenland to Ellesmere, Devon, and Baffin Islands in Canada. The purposes of our trip were to bear witness to the changes in the Arctic and get a glimpse of what a future Arctic might look like as well as to understand how people living there felt about the changes already taking place. Even before we set off, we knew that we would see signs of a new Arctic unfolding, but none of us could have imagined at the outset what we would encounter on that trip. Ice was absent from much of the eastern Arctic Ocean we sailed through that summer, but there were stranger, more surprising changes afoot, changes that seem to be occurring as a result of fundamental shifts in the ocean below us.

Orcas, which were once extremely rare in the Arctic, were chasing and killing beluga whales and narwhals off the coast of Baffin Island. Pacific salmon were being caught in Greenland and the eastern Arctic of Canada.

Even more eye-popping was a powerful cyclone that tore through the central Arctic in August, churning and breaking up sea ice cover that was already heading to a record low. Coming at a time of year when weather in the Arctic tends to be benign, this storm was remarkable in lasting nearly two weeks. Not only was it the most powerful Arctic summer storm on record, it proved to be as intense as all but thirteen of the worst winter storms seen in this part of the world.

Whichever way one looked at it, there had not been a summer in the Arctic like this one, not even in 2007 when sea ice retreated to its previous record low. And all the changes we were seeing on our voyage pointed to signs of the effects of shifting ocean currents and changes in the way that sea creatures, as well as boats, could navigate the frigid waters. It was clear that warming temperatures, melting sea ice, and changes in the way the Arctic Ocean circulates were affecting the ocean environment in several significant ways: opening up pathways for southern marine mammals to move north, allowing moisture to rise from open water and fuel violent summer storms, and making once-ice-choked channels open up and provide safe passage to vessels like ours. Once a slumbering giant that had been covered in thick ice for most of the year, the Arctic Ocean was waking up from its hypothermic state and flexing its muscle in ways that scientists are only beginning to understand.

Even with the absence of ice that was visible on the satellite maps in August, I suspected that it would not be an easy trip when I boarded our sailboat at Grise Fiord, the Arctic's northernmost community. It wasn't so much the six-hour rotations on watch that worried me nor the prospects of sharing the cooking and cleaning duties. What concerned me most were the claustrophobic conditions we were to live and work in.

The dining area was tiny, with not enough room for all seven of us on board to sit down at one time. There was no shower or hot water, and the kitchen—which had a two-burner stove and a small oven that heated only to one temperature, 450 degrees Fahrenheit—was barely big enough for one person to stand in.

I also knew that rest wouldn't come easily the moment I saw our sleeping quarters. Mine was 7 feet long, 3½ feet wide, and just 2 feet high. With my head on a pillow, there were only 3 inches of space separating my nose from the ceiling.

Getting into the bunk that first night was a bit like spelunking. I gasped for air after struggling to climb in and squeeze into this sardine can. The lingering smell of diesel that had backed up from the boat's heater didn't help, nor did the sounds and sights coming from the other three bunks.

It had been blowing snow the previous three days, and although relatively calm weather had finally arrived, there was still enough wave action in Jones Sound to make some of my colleagues queasy. Four feet across from me that first night, French biologist Sophie Chollet was in her bunk, retching violently into a paper bag. In the bunk below, Martin Von Mirbach, the Arctic program director for the World Wildlife Fund in Canada, was snoring as if he were nearing the end of life, thanks perhaps to a steady drip of Dramamine coming from a patch glued to the skin behind his ear.

Glancing over at polar bear biologist Vicki Sahanatien, I realized that it could have been worse. She was white as a ghost but holding her own, and she was probably wondering, as I was, how the four of us were going to hold up when the time came to sail into some serious weather.

As small as our yacht was, I knew that we were in good hands the moment I saw skipper Grant Redvers's resume. After an early career that had him sailing to Antarctica and South Georgia several times on a similar-sized yacht, he was given the job of heading up the 2006–2008 Tara Arctic expedition, which sought to replicate, in part, Norwegian explorer Fridtjof Nansen's remarkable attempt in 1893–1896 to get to the North Pole by harnessing powerful ocean currents that are driving some of the current changes we are now seeing take place.

Since the days when humans first began kayaking and sailing in the Arctic, it was obvious that sea ice moved, at least on a small scale. It was Nansen's voyage on the ship *Fram*, however, that demonstrated how wind and ocean currents could move this ice very rapidly over great distances.

Building on Nansen's insights, oceanographers have since shown how the main flow of Arctic water is from west to east. The inflow begins with water from the Pacific that is cold and relatively fresh entering the Arctic through the Bering Sea. This water is extremely rich in nutrients and is the main reason the Bering and Chukchi Seas are two of the most biologically productive oceans in the world.

When the frigid winter winds blowing off the coast of Alaska freeze this water and send the ice out to sea, the salt expelled from the ice dissolves into the water left behind. This heavier, salt-laden water eventually sinks and spills over the continental shelf into the Canada Basin. When it comes into contact with an Atlantic current carrying warm, saltier water through Fram Strait between Greenland and Spitsbergen, the lighter, fresher water from the west naturally settles on top. Trapped below, the denser, warmer Atlantic layer is unable to release its heat into the atmosphere.

In the Beaufort Sea, north of Alaska and the Yukon, powerful winds send this inflow of relatively fresh Pacific water spinning into an enormous gyre that circulates in clockwise fashion over a 450,000-square-kilometer area that includes a plume of fresh, nutrient-rich water fanning out from the Mackenzie River. When the winds weaken, large volumes of this freshwater circulating in the Beaufort Gyre leak out through several gateways between the islands of the Arctic Archipelago before spilling out into two main channels leading into the North Atlantic.

This circulation of surface water is like an air conditioner that moderates the northern hemisphere's climate. Any disruption in the plumbing system that drives the air conditioner not only has the potential to lead to a change in the temperature, salinity, and chemistry—and, ultimately, the marine life—in the Arctic Ocean, it can also affect the climate on a global scale by altering the path of the jet stream. Like El Niño's warm currents in the Pacific, changes in the Arctic Ocean's ice cover and circulation can exacerbate droughts in drought-stricken areas and strengthen hurricanes in areas prone to storms.

The Bering and Chukchi Seas, which separate Russia from Alaska, are showing significant signs of dramatic change, putting them on the front lines of the Arctic's transition into a new kind of ecosystem. Oceanographers such as Jackie Grebmeier and Eddy Carmack have seen the production of plankton there drop as nutrient supply from deeper waters is constrained by increased stratification associated with ice melt. With less plankton for worms, krill, shrimp, clams, and amphipods to feed on, bigger bottom-feeding species like walrus and gray whales are being forced to go farther north to find food. Cold-water fish species such as pollock and salmon are following.

The changes have already resulted in a catastrophic decline in Chinook salmon runs along the Yukon River watershed. In the seven runs from 2007 to 2012, five of them were so low that they failed to meet U.S.–Canada treaty obligations that regulate commercial harvests. The situation is so bad that the commercial harvest was canceled entirely for 2014.

No one knows whether there is a connection, but some of these salmon are now moving into Canadian waters, presumably by taking advantages of new marine pathways that appear to be opening up as sea ice retreats and ocean currents shift and warm. In recent years, Inuit, Inuvialuit, and Dene fishers in the Arctic Archipelago and in the Mackenzie, Peel, and Liard river systems have been hauling in an increasingly large number of chum and pink salmon as well as sockeye, chinook, coho, and even kokanee.

Cobourg Island was the first of several unscheduled stops on the circuitous route we took to get into the Northwest Passage from Grise Fiord. Situated at the east end of Jones Sound, the island is rugged, uninhabited, and covered at its core by glaciers. Here, after a day of taking ocean water samples for Sophie Chollet to analyze back at a lab in Great Britain, we saw none of the ice nor any of the polar bears that legendary Canadian artists Lawren Harris and A. Y. Jackson had seen in August 1930, when the captain of their ship was forced to abort an attempt to land here. Vicki Sahanatien was disappointed but not surprised considering that there was no ice to provide a platform for bears to hunt seals.

What we did see and experience were powerful winds blowing east from Greenland and getting sucked into the Canadian Arctic, perhaps linked to that powerful cyclone that had formed off the coast of Alaska in early August. Seeking shelter on the west side of the island that first night, we watched as dark, bulbous clouds swept over the cliffs of Cobourg like the Norse goddesses portrayed in John Charles Dollman's famous painting *The Ride of the Valkyries*. All that was missing that night was music by Wagner.

The great Arctic cyclone of August 2012 may have been yet another sign signaling that this slumbering giant of an Arctic Ocean is waking up and, like Boreas, the purple-winged God of the north wind, bringing a change in weather patterns.

Strong winds like those generated by this storm are very effective in transferring heat and moisture between the atmosphere and the ocean or surface of the sea ice. Scientists tracking that storm initially suspected that this one accelerated the meltdown that was already heading to a record low.

Whether that was the case is still a matter of debate. But most everyone agrees that summer storms, which appear to be on the rise in the Arctic, have the potential to break sea ice into smaller floes that will melt more quickly as the water warms. That, in turn, could disrupt sea ice and ice-edge ecosystems that currently favor beluga whales, narwhals, and the arctic cod they feed on (Figure 3.1).

Arctic cod are small fish that are as important to predators in the Arctic Ocean as lemmings and arctic ground squirrels are to arctic fox, arctic wolves, wolverine, snowy owls, and other birds of prey on the

Figure 3.1 Like narwhals, beluga whales are ice-dependent marine mammals. They feed along and under the ice edges, and they use the ice cover to protect themselves from killer whales. Photo credit: Edward Struzik

tundra. Close to a billion of these fish have been found in individual schools in Lancaster Sound, the entranceway to the Northwest Passage in Arctic Canada. Not only do arctic cod sustain narwhal and beluga, they are a key source of food for the 10 million seabirds that nest in the polar world. Scientists estimate that in Lancaster Sound alone—two days' sailing from Coburg Island—seabirds consume 23,000 metric tons of arctic cod annually. Designated a National Wildlife Area in 1995, Cobourg Island is one of the most important nesting sites in the eastern Arctic. At last count, there were 30,000 pairs of black-legged kittiwake, 160,000 pairs of thick-billed murres, and 3,000 pairs of northern fulmar nesting along its cliffsides.

Like most seabirds that nest in the Arctic, the ones that come to Cobourg time their arrival to the melting that begins to take place during the twenty-four hours of sunlight in late spring. Light passing through the thinning ice triggers a bloom of algae and zooplankton that take up carbon dioxide from seawater before transforming it to organic carbon in their tissue. The krill and copepods that thrive under the ice provide food for small fish such as arctic cod and are therefore the foundation of this ecosystem.

Sea ice in this part of the world isn't retreating as quickly as it is in Hudson Bay, however, where the spring melt is occurring three to four weeks earlier than it did thirty years ago. When it does, as it inevitably will, the effects could be serious. In Hudson Bay, capelin have already overtaken cod as the main species of fish. Murres and others seabirds that nest there now have to fly farther afield to find the food they need to get through the summer. At the same time, orcas are moving in, killing beluga whales and seals.

Although the murres appear to be adapting to the changes in diet in Hudson Bay, it's not altogether clear how birds and marine mammals will adapt at Cobourg and other parts of the Arctic. This piece of the puzzle to the future Arctic interests Inuit hunters who are having an increasingly difficult time in some places finding and getting to seals and whales because of the diminishing ice.

Times were so tough in the summer of 2012 that Inuit hunters in Greenland were killing their dogs because the absence of ice made it difficult for them to hunt the seals and whales they need to feed them as well as their families. The alternatives in the Arctic are unaffordable for most people living there. It is not unusual for residents of Grise Fiord, a day's sail from Coburg Island, to pay $15 for a head of cabbage, $4 for a single tomato, and more than $20 for the typical bag of apples one buys in a food store down south. For some store owners, it's not even worth the cost to fly fresh food in at certain times of the year because no one has the money to buy it. There was so little fresh food in Grise Fiord when we stopped at its single store that we came away with nothing but a few cartons of condensed milk to augment the supply of canned and freeze-dried food we had on hand.

As tough at it is at times for the Inuit, they greeted us politely most everywhere we went, offering fresh char to replace the canned salmon and tuna we often ate. One notable exception occurred in a tiny village near Qaanaaq, where a Greenlandic woman firmly objected to the filming of a narwhal hunt. She insisted that nothing good ever came from southerners coming to the Arctic.

I had expected a similar reception several days later when three of us hopped into the Zodiac and headed into the Inuit town of Arctic

Bay in Admiralty Inlet at the north end of Baffin Island. Several years ago, Inuit leaders here enacted a bylaw that banned tourists from visiting this community of eight hundred people. The bylaw was passed in response to a *National Geographic* article that suggested that the Inuit of Arctic Bay were wasteful in the way they hunted narwhal.

Initially, the sight of two Mounties and a government official waiting for us on shore had me thinking the worst, but if these people were still wary of outsiders like us, they didn't show it once we set foot on land. The Mounties and the government official who greeted us were simply curious about who we were, where we had come from, and where we were going. They were also offering to help in whatever way they could.

Walking around town, talking to people who stopped me in the street to find out who I was and what I was doing there, it was clear from many of the conversations that everyone was still excited by the successful bowhead whale hunt that had ended ten days earlier. It was a first for a community known more for its narwhal hunting tradition than for harvesting the much bigger bowheads.

According to Jack Willie, the Inuit manager of the hunters and trappers organization in Arctic Bay, the chase was quick, the kill was clean, and the 30-foot-long whale was cut up in just a day and a half.

At the time, Willie was at his office measuring a couple of narwhal tusks that Inuit hunter Teman Avingaq had brought in to register. A little over 6 feet long, such specimens can bring in more than $1,500 each, a lot of money in a community where there have been few jobs since the zinc mine at nearby Nanisivik shut down for good in 2002.

Narwhals are one of three whales that live in the Arctic year-round; the others are belugas and bowheads. Slightly smaller than the beluga, the narwhal has two vestigial teeth, one or both of which grow to impressive lengths in males. Narwhals that are found in Admiralty Inlet begin their journey in the waters of Greenland in springtime when the dense ice pack there begins to splinter. As narrow leads open up, they follow the retreating sea ice all the way to Lancaster Sound and beyond, presumably feeding on arctic cod, polar cod, and Greenland halibut along the way. In June, Inuit in Arctic Bay spend several days on the floe edge waiting for them to pass by in one of these leads, critical to both the narwhal's passage and the hunter's access.

These long, thin leads are formed by powerful currents and winds that push the ice around. Successful as the bowhead hunt had been that summer, 2012 had not been a good year for narwhal, which is a main driver of the local economy. Hunters had harvested only half of the 130 animals they are entitled to take under a quota system that both they and government scientists agree on. Normally, they get most of their whales off the floe edge that forms in spring, but with shifting currents and warmer temperatures, hunters are having a difficult time.

"This year that floe edge didn't materialize," Clare Kines, the local economic development officer told me. "Maybe it's global warming that was the cause. You'd be crazy to suggest that it wasn't happening. There are signs of change everywhere. Orcas are killing narwhal, and just a few days ago people here were pulling in Pacific salmon instead of arctic char."

Killer whales, I knew, have been here before. In 2005, scientists Kristin Laidre, Mads Peter Heide-Jørgensen, and Jack Orr saw a pod kill at least four narwhals in the region. I had my doubts though that the fish being netted in Arctic Bay were salmon from the Pacific until I met up with Sakiasie Qaunaq, one of three men in the community who had netted some. "I don't know what they are," he said when he showed me a few of the frozen specimens. "But they are not the fish we get here. They are different. This is the second year in a row that this has happened. It's very strange."

Qaunaq's fish weren't the only Pacific salmon that had strayed far off the beaten path that summer. Researchers from the Greenland Institute of Natural Resources caught a pink salmon off the coast of Greenland on the very day we sailed into Arctic Bay. It was the first pink salmon ever caught in west Greenland waters.

The story of how Pacific salmon made their way this far to the eastern Arctic and Greenland is one of the more striking examples of how shifting ocean currents, rising air temperatures, melting sea ice, and summer storms are playing out in the Arctic (Figure 3.2).

Oceanographer Eddy Carmack and fisheries biologist Karen Dunmall suggest that the record Arctic meltdown of 2012 may have opened up a marine pathway that allowed the fish caught in Greenland to get entrained in the transpolar drift, a current that carries water from the North Pacific across the polar cap into Greenland through Denmark

Figure 3.2 The retreat of sea ice is opening up new pathways for Pacific salmon and near-Arctic marine mammals. Photo credit: Edward Struzik

Strait. This particular salmon, they say, likely started its journey in the Lena River of Siberia where there are small natal runs of pink salmon. From there, it skirted, or actively fed, along the ice edges before arriving in east Greenland. Dunmall estimates that the 2,500–nautical mile trip took approximately 107 days, assuming that salmon are capable of swimming approximately 23.3 nautical miles per day.

The Pacific salmon that were caught in Arctic Bay, off Baffin Island, likely began their journey in the western Arctic, where kokanee, sockeye, chinook, coho, and chum salmon have been showing up in the nets of Inuit and Dene fishers in increasing numbers in the past decade. That there are chum in the western Arctic is no surprise. These fish have been found in the Colville delta and other rivers of northern Alaska for years. Both the Gwich'in and the South Slavey people who live along the Mackenzie River watershed have words— "Shii" and "łue metth'ę detsili"—for this fish, which suggests that they have probably been around for some time.

Kokanee, on the other hand, must have gotten into the Mackenzie watershed in the western Arctic by way of the Peace-Athabasca delta.

The other salmon species either overwintered somewhere in Arctic Canada or migrated from Alaska. To a rational mind, all scenarios seem unlikely.

The numbers of chum and other Pacific salmon, however, have been rising dramatically since 2003, when it was rare or unheard of to see such fish in the Arctic. Working with Canadian scientist Jim Reist, Karen Dunmall has been attempting to track salmon that people in the Arctic are catching. Those who have participated in the study reported catching forty-one pink salmon in 2004, eighteen the following year, three in 2011, and eight in 2012. During that time, they also hauled in ten sockeye, seven chinook, one coho, and one kokanee.

Carmack, from his vantage point as an oceanographer, suspects that the sockeye, chinook, coho, and pink salmon may be following warm waters that are flowing in from the Pacific and exploiting the nutrient-rich waters in those parts of the Beaufort Sea that are influenced by the freshwater coming out of the Mackenzie River.

The influence of freshwater flowing from the Mackenzie into the Arctic Ocean is enormous, capable as it is of covering 60,000 square kilometers of the shelf area in all directions to a depth of 5 meters or more. The volume of water discharging from the river is highest during spring breakup. Then, most of the river's water is impounded by landfast ice and ridges of rubble ice called stamukhi that exist at its outer edges.

The damming of the river by stamukhi results in a huge reservoir of freshwater that Carmack refers to as Lake Mackenzie. As this water in Lake Mackenzie accumulates and river flows increase, the river starts to back up and overflow its banks. Most of the overflow, however, occurs in the spring, when there is too much river water upstream squeezing through ice-covered channels that are too small to handle the volumes. Unable to withstand the intense pressure, the river ice breaks into big pieces of rubble that then jam the channels and constrict water flowing through them. Javes, as these jam-release waves are called, come from the sudden release of upstream ice jams.

Once the landfast ice and stamuhki melt, the inflow forms a plume of fresh, nutrient-rich water that tends to flow east to the Bathurst polynya, east from the mouth of the Mackenzie River, because of the Coriolis force. Presumably, those salmon that were caught in Arctic

Bay overwintered in Bathurst Inlet or somewhere nearby before following that plume of water as it headed east.

Sea ice retreat may not be good for arctic cod and other ice-edge fish species, but it has the potential to open up vast unexploited areas to salmon, Greenland halibut, mackerel, and other fish that have high commercial value. The problem is that scientists do not have data that can tell how new species will move in, what effect they will have on the food chain, and whether their numbers could support a sustainable harvest.

Commercial fish companies are nevertheless watching these climate- and ocean-current-driven changes unfold with interest. Bigger boats and advances in fishing methods have made it easier for them to capture more fish faster and farther away from port than at any time in history. Chinese factory trawlers, for example, routinely travel 7,500 miles to catch krill in and around Antarctica. A similar journey could get those trawlers into a so-called donut hole of 1.1 million square miles in the central Arctic Ocean that does not fall under any country's jurisdiction.

Fearing that industry will exploit this and other emerging resources in the Arctic, a substantial number of policy analysts, scientists, and even some commercial fishermen have successfully called for a moratorium in this donut hole. Other areas of the Arctic, however, are still vulnerable to exploitation and are in need of better fisheries management agreements.

The fear is that in a future Arctic, fishing companies will overexploit fish as they did in the 1960s through to the 1980s when Russian trawlers scooped up redfish and grenadier in Baffin Bay and Davis Strait to the point where the stocks there are now almost completely depleted. Both Barents Sea cod and Bering Sea pollock have also suffered from extreme harvesting pressures. Even with proper fisheries management in place, however, the possibility of an oil spill affecting this emerging resource is a reasonable fear.

Eddy Carmack has conducted ninety field investigations in rivers, lakes, and seas and published almost two hundred scientific articles during his long career. Having first traveled to the Arctic in 1969, the year of Woodstock, he is only half joking when he paraphrases Bob Dylan in saying that "things are a-changing" in this polar environment.

He has no doubt that new marine pathways will open the door to new species moving into the Arctic. If we are mismanaging the present, he asks, how can we hope to manage the future?

As enriched and bountiful as some parts of future Arctic may become as sea ice retreats and ocean currents shift, Carmack worries that we may be too quick in trying to exploit it, further damaging this ecological response to climate change. With competing interests and so much uncertainty, however, all parties realize that managing the future Arctic well requires dealing with many emerging questions that have no easy answers.

This truth was driven home by Arctic scientist Henry Huntington a couple of years ago when we chatted at the International Polar Year conference in Montreal. Huntington is in good company when he suggests that we will never know everything about an ecosystem or even a single species. So, the prudent things to do, he says, are to make estimates, assess our confidence in our knowledge, and act with caution.

The problem is that uncertainty is often used as an argument to forge ahead with development or exploitation rather than a reason to use caution. But there are precedents for using science to inform industry practices. Huntington points to fisheries management in Alaska and the Yukon Territory, which is based on scientific stock assessments that build in a margin of error. Fishermen there understand that long-term benefits may have short-term costs. In 1997, when salmon returns to southwest Alaska's Bristol Bay were low, managers—with the support of fishermen—curtailed the harvest despite the resulting temporary economic hardship. No one knows just how effective this ban was, but enough salmon were able to spawn in the rivers of the region to allow stocks to rebound to healthy levels, supporting an important and sustainable resource.

Whether the close of chinook salmon fishery in the Yukon River in 2014 will do the same remains to be seen. The ten-year decline there has shown no sign of abating. It may well be that climate-driven changes in the ocean are what's driving down the salmon numbers and that no moratorium can address those consequences.

The far-reaching effects of shifting currents in the Arctic are steadily becoming more noticeable to those of us above water, and they will bring even greater changes. We ourselves saw a poignant scene on the last day of our sailing trip. In the wee hours of a cold, foggy morning, a large pod of narwhals passed us, moving away from what I imagined was a pod of orcas hunting them down. The relentless east wind had calmed by then, and the cold fog that chilled us to the bone was finally lifting. But it wasn't killer whales that we saw in the faint light of the rising sun moments later. Instead, it was two big cargo ships steaming west toward Mary River on Baffin Island, where European-based steel giant Arcelor Mittal proposes to extract 18 million metric tons of iron ore by 2035.

With ice no longer being the impediment that it once was in this part of the world, mining and shipping companies are also moving in, using the same pathways that narwhals and belugas use to get to and from their winter and summering habitat. So is the military.

Anchored among the local fishing boats at Baffin Island's Pond Inlet were a Canadian warship and a U.S. Coast Guard vessel. Crew members from both ships, we discovered the next day, were walking the streets, shaking hands, and suggesting, it seemed to me, that the Inuit should get used to the idea that they will see a lot more such ships in the future. The warship, however, wasn't getting nearly as much attention from locals as were three pods of orcas that had been killing narwhals and belugas in the region.

"A week ago hunters from here killed a narwhal west of here," an Inuit man told me when I asked about the orcas. "As they were bringing it in, a killer whale came along and grabbed its tusk by the teeth. The hunter was on the other end, trying to keep it because the tusk was worth a couple of thousand dollars. But the killer whale was too strong, and the hunter eventually had to let go."

Pausing for a moment as if trying to make sense of it all, the old man simply shrugged.

Chapter 4

Stormy Arctic

The New Normal

IN THE SUMMER OF 2000, Canadian national parks warden Angus Simpson and his colleagues were camped along the north coast of Yukon Territory near the Alaskan border, conducting a survey of archeological sites along the coast. The sea was dead calm at the time, but they could see in the inky blue sky over Beaufort Sea the telltale signs of a storm advancing. An hour or so after they turned in for the night, the first big gust of wind blew in, completely flattening their tent and forcing them to take refuge in the cubbyhole of their boat.

It was just the beginning of a summer storm that some people in the western Arctic of Alaska, Yukon Territory, and Northwest Territories remember as the worst they had seen before the great cyclone of 2012 ripped through the region. At the height of this gale in 2000, dozens of Inuvialuit people camped on low-lying land along the Arctic coast had to be airlifted out by helicopter. The park wardens, exposed on the same stretch of low-lying tundra, were forced to make a harrowing trip through 12-foot-high waves to get to the safety of a ranger station that was located on Herschel Island a few miles away.

Simpson and his colleagues would have gladly stayed put at Herschel Island had it not been for an emergency satellite telephone call from an American rafter who was all alone and in distress at the mouth of the Firth River, which flows out of Alaska into the Yukon. The entire spit of land that he was camped on was quickly being submerged by high waves and a storm-driven surge of seawater. Throwing caution to the wind, Simpson and his colleagues steered their boat into the high seas that night to rescue him.

I remember the storm well because I was on the north edge of this weather system helping biologists find peregrine falcons and rough-legged hawk nests along cliffsides on the Arctic islands. When the storm hit us, we were camped on a sandy stretch of tundra. Short-lived as this storm was, it came with deafening claps of thunder and blinding flashes of lightning. Unaccustomed to violent electrical storms such as this one, dozens of musk oxen grazing in a valley nearby stampeded in one direction and then another, not knowing where the threat was coming from.

The winds whipped up so much sand that visibility was reduced to just a few feet. Looking more like warriors in a desert storm than birders on the tundra, it was all we could do that first night to prevent our small tent camp from being blown away. It was miraculous that not one of the bird nests we found in the days that followed had been destroyed.

The storm of 2000 got its start off the coast of Alaska on August 10. Sustained wind speeds of 56 miles per hour were followed intermittently by gusts that reached 65 miles per hour and more. It came on so suddenly that emergency management teams in the town of Barrow, Alaska, didn't have time to build protective berms before the storm hit.

At Barrow, the winds sunk a dredge barge, tore off the roofs of forty buildings, washed out a boat ramp, and caused $7.7 million in damage, which would have amounted to much more had the region been more populated.

By the time the storm had finished ripping through the coastal regions of the Yukon and Northwest Territories, it had completely flooded the historic whaling settlement on Herschel Island, swept several archeological sites along the coast into the sea, and left the Inuit community of Tuktoyaktuk in the Northwest Territories 10 meters closer to dropping off into ocean due to the erosion it caused on shore.

A state visit to the Inuit community of Sachs Harbour by the Queen's representative in Canada had to be canceled. The Governor General was instead forced to hunker down for a night in the small Inuit community of Ulukhaqtuuq (Holman Island) on Victoria Island.

Such severe summer storms that cause considerable damage have been relatively uncommon in the western Arctic because of high pressure and sea ice that lingers long into the summer season. With so much heat being reflected back into the atmosphere, there was not enough open water in the past to produce the moisture needed to grow cyclones with any degree of consistency.

This situation promises to change as the Arctic Ocean becomes seasonally ice-free. In the "new normal" that is opening up new pathways for killer whales and Pacific salmon to move into the Arctic, rising temperatures and disappearing sea ice are also fueling storms that used to be triggered later in autumn.

With little or no sea ice to buffer the shoreline, storm-driven surges are extending their reach several miles inland, flooding communities, killing wetlands, and accelerating the thawing of permafrost that is already eroding riverbanks and coastlines.

Climatologist Stephen Vavrus isn't convinced that the era of storminess in the Arctic is here just yet. But as detailed in a study they published in 2013, he and his colleagues at the Center for Climatic Research at the University of Wisconsin–Madison used historical climate model simulations to demonstrate that there has been an Arctic-wide decrease in sea-level pressure since the 1800s. "Simulated trends in Arctic mean sea level pressure and extreme cyclones are equivocal," says Vavrus. "Both indicate increasing storminess in some regions, but the magnitude of changes to date are modest compared with future projections."

If the recent past tells us anything about an increasingly stormy future, it's that hell comes with high water. One relatively modest storm in 1970 sent a surge of water several miles inland, killing two men who were doing maintenance on a navigation tower on the Mackenzie River in Canada. Another in the summer of 1944 tore a large strip off the shoreline of Tuktoyaktuk at the mouth of the Mackenzie delta. Two men who were there that day watched in amazement as the transport office next door to them moved once and then twice before the surge of seawater sent the building sailing, in their words, at "an even keel past the wharf and over to the island."

One of the men expected the stovepipe in the floating building to give a "cheery whistle" before the warehouse hit the island and broke up into a hundred pieces.

"You can't imagine the scene," the Hudson Bay Company employee wrote. "Diesel oil drums, gas drums, coal oil drums, full and empty crashing around and floating away, dogs, board walks, wharf and lumber, all going, water pouring into store and warehouse and into the house, the two of us trying to do a hundred jobs at once and getting desperate. The water was 12 inches deep in the warehouse, store and dwelling house. We had an inch rope round the house, between house and store the water was almost waist deep."

The difference between now and then is that rising sea levels, sinking coastlines, and receding sea ice have the potential to transport storm-driven surges even farther inland than they have gone before, sending saltwater into places where it can cause catastrophic damage. The effects range from killing tundra plants and freshwater ecosystems to accelerating erosion that is washing the land out from under native communities. Understanding how bad these storms are likely to get is key to understanding a significant element of both human and wild existence in the future Arctic.

Surges occur when winds blow over a long fetch of shallow water. The force of these winds entrains the top mass of the water column and hauls it toward shore. These surges can get particularly nasty when they occur at high tide in shallow water along low-lying coastal regions such as those in the western Arctic of North America and Arctic Russia.

In such cases, water being dragged toward the shorelines cannot descend to greater depths before it hits the coast. With nowhere else to go, it is forced up onto the land as a flood or large waves. That is what happened when Hurricane Sandy struck the northeast coast of the United States in 2012. It wasn't so much the winds that caused the estimated $50 billion in damages, but rather the 12-foot surge of water that swept inland, flooding subway lines, airport runways, and more than 650,000 homes.

In the lowest-lying parts of the western Arctic that are no more than 6 feet above sea level, this water can travel much farther than

Sandy's surge. Three storms that struck the Yukon-Kuskokwim delta in Alaska in 2005, 2006, and 2011 resulted in flooding that extended, respectively, 18.8 miles, 17 miles, and 20 miles inland. Another that swept 12.5 miles into the Mackenzie delta in 1999 killed more than 13,000 hectares of vegetation.

Damage from that surge in 1999 was unlike anything seen on that part of the Arctic coast in the last thousand years. Scientists found that more than half the alders dried up within a year of the surge. Another 37 percent of what remained shriveled in the salty soil over the next five years. A dramatic increase in the salt-loving algae *Navicula salinarum* in one inland lake suggests that the freshwater environment affected by the flooding has moved into a new and much less productive ecosystem trajectory.

"Much of it is still a dead zone," says scientist Steve Kokelj. "The saltwater intrusion changed the chemistry of the lakes and the soil in a very fundamental way. What little has come in to replace it is nothing like what was once there. We didn't get a chance to assess the impact on wildlife, but local Inuvialuit hunters tell us that both moose and geese are no longer using the areas to the extent that they did in the past."

The storm surges that swept into the Mackenzie and the Yukon-Kuskokwim deltas may be considered extraordinary now, particularly for the length of their reach, but such storms are bound to become more common as sea levels rise, storms pick up steam, and the western Arctic continues, literally, to sink. Unlike western Hudson Bay, which is rebounding from the heavy weight of glaciers that compressed the landscape for tens of thousands of years, the more lightly glaciated regions of the western Arctic of Canada, Alaska, and Arctic Russia are subsiding at a time when sea levels are rising.

In the past, sea ice that prevailed long into the summer protected these low-lying Arctic shorelines from the full effect of these surges. Offshore floes, for example, shorten the length of those fetches of water that are necessary for the top mass of the water column to build momentum. Closer to shore, landfast ice and stamukhi often blunted the force of big waves.

The presence of sea ice could be one reason why that storm surge in 1970 didn't cause more damage than it did. Scientists who reconstructed events that led up to the storm noted that pack ice, which covered a tenth to more than a half of the ocean 12.5 miles seaward, may have accounted for the relatively small 9-foot-high waves that were observed.

The effect of all this relatively warm, salty water coming onto shore is exacerbated by the 50 to 70 percent of the soil along western Arctic coastlines that consists of frozen water, a "dirty iceberg" as geomorphologist Robert Anderson of the University of Colorado Boulder describes it. Once it comes into contact with the warmer water, it falls apart and slips into the sea.

Anderson and other researchers believe that as the Arctic Ocean becomes increasingly ice-free, storm surges will affect ever-larger areas of shoreline in the Arctic basin. Included is Russia's immense Arctic coastline, which stretches many thousands of miles.

In association with German and Russian colleagues, Frank Günther, a scientist with the Alfred Wegener Institute in Germany, has been investigating the causes of the coastal breakdown in eastern Siberia. In 2013, he and his colleagues reported that summer temperatures that have risen dramatically have exacerbated this breakdown. Between 1951 and 2012, for example, temperatures in the region exceeded the freezing point an average of 110 days. In 2010 and 2011, they did so 127 times. In 2012, the warmest year on record in the Arctic, it happened 134 times.

Over the past two decades, the number of ice-free days averaged 80 per year. In 2012, there were 96 ice-free days that significantly accelerated the erosion that is already taking place.

Günther predicts that sometime within this century the island of Muostakh, which is east of the Siberian harbor town of Tiski, will break into several sections and then disappear altogether.

Even now, hundreds of thousands of tons of plant-, animal-, and microorganism-based carbon are washed into the sea along every mile of eroding coastline each year. These materials had previously been sealed in the permafrost. Günther and his colleagues predict that this accelerated erosion will have an effect on the chemistry of the Arctic Ocean. Once in the water, carbon may turn into carbon dioxide and, as a result, contribute to the acidification of the oceans.

In Arctic Canada and Alaska, the story is much the same. Benjamin

Jones of the U.S. Geological Survey (USGS) recently found that a stretch of coastline he had been monitoring in Alaska had retreated an average of 22.3 feet per year between 1955 and 1979. Over the next twenty-three years, that rate increased by 28 percent. The low-lying coastline of Alaska that Jones was studying was losing 44.6 feet of land per year between 2002 and 2007 and 82 feet between 2008 and 2009.

The effect of this loss is exacerbated by rapid permafrost thawing occurring farther upstream along big Arctic rivers such as the Yukon and Mackenzie. Steve Kokelj and his colleagues have documented monumental slumpings of riverbanks in the Peel River that flows from the Yukon into the Northwest Territories into the Mackenzie. The collapse of these shorelines changes both the chemistry of the rivers and the shoreline soils in a way that may be lethal to fish and favorable for invasive plants species that are migrating north and over-taking some tundra ecosystems.

All these changes have implications for Inuit communities as well as Arctic ecosystems (Figure 4.1). In 2006, I accompanied the late Ca-nadian coastal geologist Steve Solomon in the field. He brought along a computer model that simulated what would happen to the town of Tuktoyaktuk if a powerful storm such as one that occurred in 2000 hit the community in 2050 when sea levels will be higher. Not only would a future storm like that one flood many parts of the commu-nity, it would also sever almost all access to the airport and prevent air evacuation if required. It would also put the community's supply of freshwater in peril.

The prospects are even more serious for Alaska because there are many more communities at risk. The U.S. Army Corps of Engineers (COE), for example, estimates that at least sixty coastal and river vil-lages in Alaska face erosion problems that will cost several hundred billions of dollars in engineering costs to mitigate. The most famous of them is Shishmaref, a native community of 625 Inupiat people who have become what some journalists have described as "climate change refugees" even though they have not yet been forced to relocate.

Often portrayed as a community on the front line of rising sea levels and coastal erosion, the island is losing 5 to 10 feet of coastline each year and as much as 100 feet or so in years when powerful storms sweep in.

Figure 4.1 Subsistence hunting will be increasingly difficult for the indigenous people who depend on marine mammals in the Arctic to provide them with food and materials for clothing. Photo credit: Edward Struzik

Over the years, there have been several attempts to shore up the town. In 2004, the Bureau of Indian Affairs (BIA) installed 200 feet of protection along the shoreline near the Native American store. The following year, the COE installed 230 feet of protection, connecting to the BIA project, extending to the east to protect the Shishmaref School. That same year, the community of Shishmaref installed about 250 feet of protection extending to the east from the COE project.

The latest plan to shore up the community is estimated to cost $25 million. The investment, however, won't be providing long-term returns. According to the COE in 2009, the "complete failure of useable land" in Shishmaref could occur in fewer than ten years (2019); at best, the community has twenty-five years (2034) left in its current location.

Other than curbing greenhouse gas emissions, there are not many solutions to the erosion problems that coastal and river communities face. Governments can either spend a lot of money on engineering solutions, or they can relocate the communities to higher, safer sites.

In Shishmaref's case, relocation would cost, by one estimate, $183 million.

As practical and cost-effective as relocation may be in the long term, it is a sensitive issue for many indigenous people, especially for those who come from families that were forced into exile in the past. As the relocation of Inuit to Ellesmere and Cornwallis Islands in Arctic Canada has shown, these relocations can either end badly or have lasting repercussions.

The practice of relocating Arctic people got its start at the end of the nineteenth century when both whalers and fur traders used alcohol, tea, tobacco, and trinkets to lure Eskimos, Inuit, the Nenet, and Chukotkans to more manageable trading centers. Willing to move as many of these indigenous people may have been at the time, they suffered the consequences. Initially, it was disease and alcoholism that ravaged their numbers. Then, when the whalers and fur traders left, leaving various Arctic regions with greatly diminished wildlife populations, a number of communities had to be abandoned.

In the ensuing decades, the relocation of indigenous northerners became far more systematic and draconian. In Arctic Russia, whaling and walrus-hunting villages were uprooted to make way for mines and military bases and to supply cheap labor for state-run reindeer farms, fishing collectives, mines, and transportation projects. Invariably, families were split up and children were sent to residential schools, often against the wishes of the parents. Many of them never came back.

The Canadians and Russians weren't the only ones who forcibly relocated indigenous northerners. In Greenland, the Danish government relocated several Inuit communities in the 1950s for various reasons. The entire village of Thule, for example, was moved 60 miles to the north in 1953 to make room for a U.S. military base.

This pattern in public policy decision making continued for decades. Whenever sovereignty, security, and economic priorities came into play, environmental integrity and the cultural interests of indigenous people in the Arctic invariably suffered.

The failure to sufficiently inform and collaborate with indigenous northerners was one reason a plan to relocate the people of Aklavik in the Mackenzie delta to a new modern Arctic town (Inuvik) was not entirely successful in the 1960s. Severe erosion, flooding, and sewage problems made relocation to a completely new town seem like a good idea to federal government officials at the time. Residents of Aklavik, however, only heard about the proposal via the local radio station after it was a done deal. Remaining true to a "never say die" motto, many of them refused to leave when it was time to go. Since then, the people of Aklavik have suffered through several more devastating floods, and still no one wants to leave.

These people are not blind to the threats and challenges that climate change brings, however. Several years ago, the community embarked on a project that sought to find out what climate change effects elders and hunters were seeing firsthand on the land and on the water. Those who responded noted that the spring melt was occurring earlier and that the autumn freeze-up was much later. They reported seeing lots of moose in the delta but fewer caribou. Caribou, they thought, were having a hard time finding food. Most everyone agreed that the weather was much harder to predict.

Local initiatives such as this project have gone a long way in getting indigenous northerners to trust scientists and decision makers. In Old Crow, a small Gwich'in town in the northern Yukon, the Vuntut people recognized some time ago that climate change threatened their very existence. Caribou were on the decline, some bird species were dwindling or disappearing, and many of the twenty-five hundred lakes in the Old Crow Flats were drying up or changing chemistry. To find the answers to the many changes that they were seeing, community leaders opened the door to hydrologists, permafrost specialists, and wildlife scientists to work with them to find the answers.

Many of those answers, however, aren't coming quickly enough, in part because government funding for Arctic research in North America is in relatively short supply compared with what is available in other countries, such as Norway and even Germany. Increasingly, observing systems, which are few and far between in the Canadian Arctic, are being automated, which means that there are fewer people on the ground actually making observations. It also means that although data are being collected from a very few sites, it is not necessarily being analyzed.

Important work is still being done by organizations such as the Arctic Institute of Community-Based Research, which focuses in part on the implications of climate change on indigenous people living in Yukon Territory, Northwest Territories, and Nunavut. In most cases, though, the Canadian government is choosing to focus on economic development rather than on the long-term threats that climate change is presenting to communities and ecosystems.

Even though the hamlet of Tuktoyaktuk is sliding into the sea, for example, more than $300 million is being spent on an all-weather gravel road to connect the community to the south. By one of the government's own accounts, the economic benefits to the community will be modest: $1.5 million in transportation savings and an estimated $2.7 million annually in tourism dollars.

The biggest return on investment will go to energy producers who stand to save $385 million in transportation costs over a forty-five-year period if a natural gas pipeline is built along the Mackenzie River valley.

Both the road and the pipeline have environmental implications that extend beyond the right-of-way. In the event that the $16 billion natural gas pipeline is built, Imperial Oil and Shell Canada, two of the pipeline proponents, have plans to develop the Taglu and Niglintgak gas fields in the Kendall Island Migratory Bird Sanctuary, which is nesting ground for many of the more than one hundred species of migratory birds present in the Mackenzie delta.

No more than 5 feet above sea level, the sanctuary is already vulnerable to sea level declines, Arctic storms surges, and the lingering effects of seismic lines that were cut in the past. Even industry concedes that extracting gas from the sanctuary, which resource companies are allowed to do in Canadian bird and wildlife sanctuaries, will make it even more vulnerable as land subsides after the natural gas is pumped out. One study suggests that as much as 1,200 hectares of bird habitat will be lost irrespective of what happens when sea levels rise and Arctic storms pick up steam.

The sum of $300 million that is being invested in building the gravel road to Tuktoyaktuk would have gone a long way toward funding research to answer many of the so-called questions that are emerging in the western Arctic as sea levels rise, storms increase, and permafrost thaws, but instead of investing in the future, the Canadian government continues to reduce the budget for Arctic science. In

2012, it ended funding for the Canadian Foundation for Climate and Atmospheric Sciences, which had doled out more than $100 million in research funding in the previous decade. And despite committing to the construction of a new Arctic research station, it has eliminated funding for a program that helps keep more than a dozen existing Arctic science research stations operational (Figure 4.2).

That funding is not likely to recover from what critics across the political spectrum say is an unprecedented assault by the Conservative government of Canadian Prime Minister Stephen Harper on environmental regulation, oversight, and scientific research. Harper, who came to power in 2006 unapologetic for once describing the Kyoto climate accords as "essentially a socialist scheme to suck money out of wealth-producing nations," has steadily been weakening environmental enforcement, monitoring, and research while at the same time boosting controversial oil sands development, backing major pipeline construction, and increasing energy industry subsidies. Each year, he travels to the Arctic without even acknowledging how climate change is affecting this part of the world more than it is elsewhere.

He and his government have gone to extraordinary lengths to make sure that it does not become a political issue. Invariably, Canadian government scientists I tried to talk to about climate change in the Arctic were unable to share their research because they are not allowed to talk to the media. Those who were willing did so from home telephone numbers and on the condition that they not be quoted. As bad as that was, it got even worse when the Canadian government sent out handlers at the 2012 International Polar Year conference in Montreal to make sure that Environment Canada scientists didn't talk to the media unless government representatives were on hand to monitor what they said.

Canada could learn a lesson from the United States, where the North Pacific Research Board and the National Science Foundation invested $52 million between 2007 and 2012 to support more than a hundred scientists who studied a range of issues in the Bering Sea. The scientists looked at everything from atmospheric forcing and physical oceanography to the effect that changing ecosystems are having on humans and the economy. More recently, the U.S. Fish and Wildlife Service, the USGS, the National Oceanic and Atmospheric

Figure 4.2 Funding for climate change science in Arctic Canada has suffered in recent years as a result of government cutbacks and the muzzling of scientists. Photo credit: Edward Struzik

Administration (NOAA), and university scientists launched several initiatives to better understand the effect of Arctic weather and changing climate on communities, migratory bird habitats, and mid-latitude zones of the United States, where weather extremes have become common in recent years. In 2014, for example, NOAA launched a five-year plan to improve management and stewardship of Alaska's marine and coastal resources, provide better sea ice and weather forecasts, and work with international organizations such as the Arctic Council. In another example, the USGC has embarked on several initiatives that aim to determine rates of coastal erosion on a decadal basis, the frequency and magnitude of storm surges, the effects of saltwater intrusion on permafrost and freshwater wetlands, and the likely consequences of these environmental changes on birds and wildlife.

Craig Ely, a USGS wildlife biologist who has been conducting bird studies in the Yukon-Kuskokwim delta, is, by way of example, trying to determine which species in the delta could be winners and which losers in a climate change scenario. If the losers become threatened or endangered, he says, measures could be taken to limit subsistence and sports hunting or to find ways to safeguard the most critical habitats.

In some ways, the road map to the future is being paved by the work that the three Landscape Conservation Cooperatives in Alaska are doing. In each case, local communities are working with scientists to develop and apply ecosystem models that are capable of forecasting how landscapes might change as the climate heats up. Scientists like David McGuire of the USGS/University of Alaska Climate Science Center are looking at everything from coastal erosion and glacial retreat to tundra and forest fires and how they may affect hydrology, species migration, tree-line advance, and vegetation changes.

Theoretically, these ecosystem models will help land and resources managers, subsistence hunters, and coastal communities make informed decisions when it comes to building roads, homes, pipelines, mines, and airport runways. They will also help when fighting fires and establishing catch-and-bag limits for fish and wildlife species.

Looking at the big picture and what's at stake, it's not a big investment. It is costing Canada $300 million to build a road to Tuktoyaktuk. It is costing Northwest Boreal Landscape Conservation Cooperative, the USGS, the Alaska Climate Science Center, and the Western

Alaska Landscape Conservation Cooperative a little less than $3 million to create and operate the Integrated Ecosystem Model for Alaska from 2010, the year it went into the pilot project phase, through 2015. The project will have additional funding to carry it through to its end in August 2016.

Time to do something, of course, is running out. Rapidly unfolding events in the Arctic will soon overwhelm the ability of decision makers to do anything meaningful about rising sea levels, coastal erosion, and powerful storms that are extending their reach farther and farther inland. Not only is the Arctic heating up faster than climate modelers previously predicted, the Arctic itself is opening the door to oil and gas development and commercial shipping that will further complicate the situation.

The problem is that governments are by nature averse to risk, except perhaps when it comes to promoting oil and gas developments in the Arctic. The road to Tuktoyaktuk may crumble as the permafrost beneath it thaws in the coming years, but the pipeline will have likely been built by that time. In contrast, seawater intrusions that come with storm surges will destroy communities and wetlands in which millions of birds nest. From both an economic and environmental perspective, it makes better sense to invest a modest amount now to avert or deal with more costly crises in the future.

Chapter 5

The Arctic Melting Pot

I N THE LATE SUMMER OF 2011 when I was hiking along the north coast of Banks Island in the High Arctic with scientist John England, we came upon the freshly excavated den of a bear. Assuming that it was one of a number of polar bears known to den in this part of the Arctic, we circled back to make sure that we weren't being stalked. Although we saw no sign of the bear anywhere on the treeless tundra, we did find the fresh tracks of the animal that had been doing the digging. The tracks, however, were not those of a polar bear. They were clearly those of a grizzly bear, presumably one that England had seen a few weeks earlier while flying over a tiny, treeless island off the northwest coast of Banks.

What this brown bear was doing along the northernmost edges of the kingdom of its white cousin is not entirely clear. Considering the time of year and the amount of effort the animal had expended digging this big hole into the frozen hillside, though, it was obvious that it had no intention of walking back to where it had come from on the mainland 300 miles to the south.

Helicoptering back to our tent camp that night, England couldn't resist the idea of carrying on to see if the bear that he had seen weeks earlier was still there on that island. It was no surprise to us that it wasn't. Evidently, however, a bull caribou had swum out this way, spooked or chased perhaps by the bear when the bear had swum back to Banks Island. Down there, the caribou looked awfully lonely and very much out of place on a small pancake of land that was no larger than the size of two football fields.

Barren-ground grizzlies are common in the western Arctic, but until about twenty years ago, sightings of grizzlies in the Arctic Archipelago were extremely rare. This quirk of nature, many biologists thought, may have simply occurred because the bear ended up walking the wrong way or strayed too far following mainland caribou that sometimes cross the sea ice to the Arctic islands. That thinking, however, began to change in recent years as more brown bears and a succession of other animals such as red fox, Pacific salmon, and killer whales began showing up in Arctic and sub-Arctic areas traditionally occupied by polar bears, Arctic fox, Arctic char, and narwhals (Figure 5.1).

The migration of southern animals into the Arctic is an intriguing development that may result in an addition or subtraction of several pieces to the puzzle that will determine what the Arctic will look like in fifty to one hundred years. The new dynamics will include the possibility of displacement of Arctic native species, with fish and animals like Pacific salmon and red fox potentially outcompeting Arctic char and Arctic fox for food and territory. And with sea ice no longer stopping them in the future, killer whales could drive beluga whales and narwhals out of the biological hotspots they depend on in summer. Additional effects could come from diseases carried by some of these southern animals from which some Arctic animals have no immunity. There is also the potential for a variety of closely related animals—such as grizzlies and polar bears—to interbreed and produce hybrids that could drive some native species to extinction. It's impossible to predict how each of these influences will shape the species that survive in the future Arctic and which ones will not, but we are already seeing evidence of change in a variety of ways.

The first time I heard of animals interbreeding in the Arctic was in the spring of 2006 when I was flying in a small plane from Tuktoyaktuk to Inuvik in the western Arctic. I had just spent a few days with scientist Ian Stirling, who was catching and tagging polar bears in the

Figure 5.1 Scientist Mark Edwards extracts a tooth from a grizzly bear that he and Andrew Derocher captured along the Arctic coast. The barren-ground grizzly population is likely to do well in a warming Arctic world. Photo credit: Edward Struzik

Beaufort Sea. After learning what I had been up to, the pilot told me that an American hunter had shot a strange-looking bear on the sea ice just west of Banks Island a week earlier. The bear apparently had the features of both a grizzly bear and a polar bear. The wildlife officer who investigated was so confused that he seized the dead animal until the origins of its parentage could be proved.

As convincingly as the pilot told the story, I still filed it away with the many tall tales I had heard from various people during my travels to the Arctic. Grizzly bears and polar bears have produced hybrids in zoos, but the biology and behavior of the two animals suggested that they would likely make war, not love, in the rare event they met on the sea ice.

In Inuvik, I didn't bother to drop in at the government wildlife office to see if there was truth to anything the pilot had told me. I soon regretted that I hadn't. Back home a few days later, I received an e-mail from polar bear biologist Andrew Derocher. With it was a link to an internal government report that described how an American hunter had indeed shot a polar bear/grizzly cross that spring (Figure 5.2). (A DNA test conducted by wildlife genetic experts months later confirmed it was a hybrid, with a polar bear mother and a grizzly bear father.)

As it was a first in the modern wild, no one was willing to suggest that this hybrid might signal a trend. It did, however, get Alaska biologist Brendan Kelly wondering whether this kind of hybridization was occurring in other Arctic species.

At the time, Kelly had thirty years of experience studying the ecology and behavior of ice-associated marine mammals in the Arctic and Antarctica. He was well aware that seals, walruses, and sea lions are more prone to hybridization because they share the same number of chromosomes, which allows them to produce offspring. He also knew that the zones in which hybridization are likely to occur have been limited by sea ice that effectively prevents Atlantic walruses and narwhals, for example, from moving into the Pacific and prevents Pacific salmon and other marine animals from moving into the eastern Arctic.

If you removed continent-sized ice sheets that prevented southern marine mammals from moving north into the Bering and Chukchi Seas and from the Bering and the Chukchi into the Arctic Archipelago, he wondered, what might be the outcome? The question was not an outlandish one because Arctic sea ice receded to a record low in 2007 when Kelly was thinking through this concept. By summer's end that year, ice cover at its minimum was 22 percent, or 459,000 square miles, smaller than it had been at the start of the melting season. That's nearly twice the size of the state of Texas. Put another way, it was a little more than 40 percent below the 1978–2000 average summer minimum.

Kelly collaborated with biologists David Tallmon of the University of Alaska and Andrew Whiteley of the University of Massachusetts Amherst to begin looking for answers to these questions about hybridization. In a review of the scientific literature, they learned that hybridization had already occurred between harp and hooded seals, narwhals and beluga whales, and very likely between North Pacific right whales and bowhead whales. Looking at the potential for more of this hybridization to happen, they concluded that at least twenty-two

Figure 5.2 This grizzly bear/polar bear hybrid was spotted in the High Arctic by biologists Jodie Pongracz and Evan Richardson in 2012. The sightings of three grizzly bears and one other hybrid that spring represented an unprecedented cluster of these animals at such high latitudes. Photo credit: Jodie Pongracz, Environment and Natural Resources, Government of the Northwest Territories

Arctic marine mammals are at risk and that many of these species—fourteen in all—are threatened or endangered.

Hybridization—the crossbreeding that takes place between two species—is more common than most scientists once thought. The frequency of interbreeding species is 25 percent in British ducks, 10 percent in birds, 6 percent in European mammals, and 12 percent in European butterflies. In the wonderfully documented case of Darwin's finches in the Galapagos, Princeton University's Rosemary Grant and Peter Grant found that hybridization occurs rarely—in less than 2 percent of breeding pairs—but persistently from year to year.

Since the days of Charles Darwin, evolutionary biologists have tried to decipher the mechanisms that prevent, or allow, species to interbreed. Among the first to speculate in a meaningful way was American Carl Hubbs, who was a professor and curator of fish, reptiles, and amphibians at various American museums and universities from 1917 to 1979, when he died.

According to his zoologist son Clark, Hubbs's surveys of freshwater fishes of North America usually involved a long car trip that included a graduate student and, later on, his own children. An "allowance" to the children was based on the number of species collected (5 cents each), with special awards for new species ($1) or new genera ($5). Fortunately, Clark recalls, his father was a "splitter" who liked to divide things into small groups as opposed to a "lumper" who groups plants and animals into broader categories. Thus, they obtained frequent "special awards."

In his studies of these collections, Carl Hubbs noted the presence of hybrids (for which the children got no special allowance). These hybrids, he deduced from his field notes and other like studies, were most likely to be found in disturbed environments, in ecosystems in which one of the parental species had been introduced, and in ecosystems in which one parental species was rare and the other abundant.

Until recently, none of these situations applied to the Arctic in any significant way. The landscape has been isolated and covered in ice, with its climate in a relatively steady state. Humans have introduced no new species. And zones of hybridization, in which one parental species is rare and the other abundant, are few and far between. In this frigid but splendid isolation, most Arctic animals evolved in their own sweet way, relatively unencumbered by fierce competition or surprise intrusions.

One can see how this scenario has influenced the evolution of Arctic wolves on Banks Island, where wolves are isolated not only by open water that separates them from mainland wolves in summer and fall, but by the presence of musk oxen (and previously caribou), which are so numerous on Banks that there is little reason for them to leave. Although Banks Island wolves are genetically similar to their cousins that inhabit Victoria Island next door, they are distinct from mainland wolf populations across the Amundsen Gulf.

A similar thing is happening with lake trout in Great Bear Lake, which sits on the Arctic Circle in the Northwest Territories in Canada. Great Bear is the eighth largest lake in the world, and it is unaffected directly by modern industrial development. It is 200 miles long, 108 miles wide, and 1,500 feet deep in some places. Many of its fish, including a 72 pounder that was caught in 2011, grow to world-record sizes.

Like most Arctic lakes, Great Bear was created thousands of years ago when the continental ice sheets retreated. Lake trout and other forms of char living in recently deglaciated regions gradually moved in to exploit the new source of food that became available. With very little competition for these new food resources, the trout ended up dividing the lake like a pie. While some became small bottom feeders, others became big bottom feeders. Such monster fish became fish eaters and occasionally cannibals. They all, more or less, exploited plankton.

Unlike most other fish species in crowded southern lakes where competition for food is intense and the ability to specialize is limited, Great Bear's trout seem to be on the same kind of fast-forward evolutionary trajectory seen in Darwin's finch in the Galapagos. Finches there evolved to have a smaller beak within two decades.

Great Bear's fish have not been evolving nearly as quickly, but working with Canada Fisheries and Oceans scientist Jim Reist, biologist Louise Chavarie has shown that in a relatively short period of time, these fish have morphed into anatomically distinct forms with different food preferences and growth rates. Although they already exhibit some genetic differences, they can still interbreed.

Interbreeding between two distinct species can be both good and bad for biodiversity. It can be good because it can lead to the evolution of new and more robust species such as the polar bear that is the product of interbreeding between prehistoric polar bears and female brown bears that crossed paths in Ireland during the Ice Age. It can be bad, however, because it can result in hybrids that are less productive or infertile, or genetically unequipped to tolerate disease and rapid environmental changes, than the original species.

This negative result is exhibited by lake trout and brook trout that have bred naturally in one small part of northern Ontario and with the help of scientists in other places. Called splake, the offspring of this interbreeding is genetically stable, but the fish has shown little success in reproducing outside a hatchery.

This kind of interbreeding can be particularly bad for threatened species such as the spotted owl, which is increasingly mating with the barred owl in the United States. Scientists have found that hybrids that are produced by interbreeding mate less frequently with the spotted owl than spotted owls would normally do with their own kind. Those that do mate with spotted owls tend to produce fewer young than those that mate with barred owls. These factors combine to increase the spotted owl's prospects of extinction.

Interbreeding also has implications for ocean species, namely the critically endangered Northern Pacific right whale. There are currently no more than two hundred left in the wild. If they interbreed with bowhead whales, as it appears that at least one has, the path to their extinction may accelerate.

Canadian scientist Jim Leafloor has contemplated how hybridization may unfold in western Hudson Bay where cackling geese and Canada geese overlap. Cackling geese and Canada geese are so similar that they were once considered to be the same species. Cacklers, however, are genetically distinct and tend to be much smaller than Canada geese and, in some cases, as small as mallards.

For hybridization to occur between Canada geese and cackling geese, the geese would have to be together at the time that mates are chosen or at the time of breeding. Unlike some species of geese, Canada geese of both sexes are known to be philopatric to their natal areas, usually returning to nest in the same general area where they were hatched themselves.

This fact led Leafloor and others to believe that Canada geese usually paired with familiar individuals from the same general nesting area. This thought makes the possibility that these two species might interbreed seem unlikely because the nesting areas would also need to be zones of overlap in which hybridization might occur. Nesting overlap, however, was not known to exist anywhere in the sub-Arctic or Arctic world. Canada geese tend to nest earlier in the boreal forest before heading north to moult. Cackling geese, on the other hand, tend to nest later on the tundra, not in the forest.

Leafloor suspected that something was amiss with this assumption when he and other scientists identified birds on the west coast of Hudson Bay that had the large body size of a Canada goose but the DNA of a cackler. In other cases, they found small birds that looked like cacklers but that had the DNA of a Canada goose. Leafloor believes that the persistence of Canada goose DNA sequences among small-bodied geese in the Arctic may be the "ghost" of historical hybridization events that occurred when the Arctic was warmer and when the tree line was farther north a few thousand years ago.

This ghost of hybridization has the potential to come back to life in the coming decades. Two possibilities will contribute to it: if the tree line continues its current northward migration and if more southern birds continue to overshoot their migration north and find new nesting sites, sites that may not have been suitable thirty years ago when the Arctic was much colder.

Like snow geese, Canada geese have expanded well beyond their historic range. In western Greenland where Canada geese were extremely rare in the 1980s, the population has risen to about fifty thousand nesting pairs. Geese there are doing so well that their clutch sizes are larger than those of Canada geese nesting 800 miles to the south. In the eastern Arctic of Canada, Canada geese are now nesting on the northeast coast of Baffin Island, 300 miles north of what was once thought to be their range limit in the eastern Arctic of Canada. As Canada geese expand their nesting ranges, the potential for hybridizing with cackling geese becomes ever more likely.

There is, however, a big difference between what has happened in the past and what is likely to happen in the future Arctic. This explosion of Canada geese and especially snow geese is as much climatically driven as it is triggered by agricultural and urban developments in the south. Vast wetlands and forest environments in the southern United States that were once unsuitable for overwintering geese have been transformed into farmers' fields that leave enormous amounts of wasted grains for geese to feed on. Energized by this newfound source of food, geese fly north to nest in larger numbers and in better shape than they were before this agricultural transformation took place. They also find sufficient vegetation to sustain them through the return flight back south thanks to the rapidly warming climate in the Arctic that makes their food sources more abundant.

Scientists are now seeing a similar story emerging with white-tailed deer and moose that are now moving into the Arctic. Unlike woodland caribou, deer and moose do well in southern environments that are fragmented by oil, gas, and forestry developments. Migrating north along cutlines and pipeline rights-of-way, these animals are no longer stopped short by brutally long winters in the Arctic.

In this case, one thing leads to another. As deer and moose numbers expand into the Arctic, southern predators such as coyotes and cougars are following. Having lived in the Yukon and Northwest Territories in the 1970s, I found that hard to believe until a pilot and a biologist I knew confidently reported seeing cougars in separate incidents, one in the Kluane ice fields near the Alaska Yukon border and the other in Wood Buffalo National Park.

Deer aren't going to be coupling with caribou, but there's the possibility that their predators, coyote and wolves, will interbreed as they have in eastern North America. Coyotes are now such a common sight in northern cities such as Yellowknife and Whitehorse that wildlife officers often advise people there to keep their small dogs inside at night.

This ecological hodgepodge of interbreeding species, shifting ranges, and competition is complicated by another, often overlooked, factor: disease. Southern animals bring with them diseases that are largely absent from the Arctic. The possibility of that happening came to light several years ago when Canadian scientists were monitoring the spread of trichonella in the Arctic. The roundworm, which is commonly found in polar bears and Arctic fox, was of little concern in the Arctic until the 1980s, when it began to spread to walrus and to humans who had eaten uncooked meat. Symptoms include fever, myalgia, malaise, and edema.

Ole Nielsen, a microbiologist working for the Canadian Department of Fisheries and Oceans, was assigned the task of tracking the spread of this parasite and determining whether there might be anything else of concern in the hunter-killed samples he was given. Initially, he was not altogether surprised to find some evidence of brucellosis, which has been linked to reproductive failure in dolphins and baleen whales. The disease is extremely widespread in the marine world, and it wasn't a stretch of the imagination to think that it might have gotten a foothold in the Arctic.

What did surprise him was the speed with which the disease has spread since he began sampling more than two decades ago. He now sees it in 21 percent of the samples that he tests, which is a fourfold increase from what he saw in the 1980s.

A bigger concern, however, was the discovery that neither beluga whales nor narwhals have antibodies that would help them resist phocine distemper, a deadly virus that was first discovered in the marine environment in 1988 when it killed twenty thousand harbor seals in northwestern Europe. Since then, it has spread to seals in Lake Baikal, striped dolphins in the Mediterranean, and several species in other places of the world.

No one knows how phocine distemper made its way into the ocean, but because it is so closely related to canine distemper, it is thought to have its origins in land-based species whose remains were dumped into saltwater. "There are a lot of unknowns should distemper make its way to the North American Arctic," says Nielsen. "If distemper gets a foothold here, it could get ugly. With there being as many as 80,000 narwhal and 150,000 belugas in the North American Arctic for most if not all of the year, a massive die-off somewhere is not out of the question."

A die-off isn't as outlandish as it might seem. All that's required is a carrier such as a pilot whale, a harbor seal, or a dolphin, all marine mammals that are known to carry the virus for long periods of time before suffering the symptoms. Any number of them could ride one of those warm currents into the Arctic just as Pacific salmon and killer whales are already doing.

Humans are not immune to the threats of spreading diseases either. In the winter of 2014, scientists reported finding, for the first time, an infectious form of the cat parasite *Toxoplasma gondii* in beluga whales that inhabit the Mackenzie delta and western Arctic waters in summer. Also known as kitty litter disease, toxoplasmosis is the leading cause of infectious blindness in humans. It can be fatal to fetuses and to people with compromised immune systems.

In reporting the results of this study, Michael Grigg and Stephen Raverty also described a new strain of a parasite in the Arctic that was responsible for killing 406 gray seals in the North Atlantic in 2012. *Sarcocystis pinnipedi* is not harmful to humans, but it has resulted in the deaths of Steller sea lions, seals, Hawaiian monk seals, walruses, polar bears, and grizzly bears in Alaska and British Columbia.

David Tallmon, one of the University of Alaska biologists looking into Arctic hybrids, sees diseases as a very real threat in a future Arctic.

But he also believes that a low level of hybridization is not necessarily a bad thing and that some good can come from interbreeding in the wild. Diversity loss, he believes, may be minor if it's simply the occasional Pacific minke interbreeding with North Atlantic minke. It's more of a concern, he says, when the interbreeding involves a threatened or endangered animal like the North Pacific right whale or if interbreeding becomes a frequent rather than a rare event.

Like his coresearcher Brendan Kelly, Tallmon believes that there are other things to consider, such as interbreeding that may have social implications. The beluga/narwhal cross that was discovered in Greenland several years ago, for example, lacked the tusk of the narwhal that is so important in breeding success. In zoos, grizzly bear/polar bear crosses exhibit the seal-hunting behavior of a polar bear but not the animal's strong swimming skills.

"There is something to be said about species adapting to climate change," Kelly told me, four years after he and his colleagues made their controversial views on hybridization known in the journal *Nature*. "But the kind of adaptation that's necessary is a shift to genes that fit the new climatic environment better than the old genes. That takes time. The change that is taking place in the Arctic now is happening so fast that long-lived animals like whales, seals, and polar bears aren't getting the chance to adapt as quickly as it is necessary."

Kelly and Tallmon had hoped that the commentary they published in *Nature* would have led to some serious discussions in the scientific community and perhaps some policy decisions at the political and bureaucratic level. Those discussions did occur. Nothing amounted to much on the policy front, however.

All three scientists still believe that the International Union for the Conservation of Nature should develop a comprehensive policy for managing hybrids, including determining when it is practical to prevent or limit hybridizations. Red wolf and coyote hybrids, by way of example, have been culled in the United States in the past decade to help preserve distinct species. They also believe that researchers should combine models of sea ice loss, oceanography, and landscape genomics to predict when and where hybridization is most likely to occur and to monitor the genetics of at-risk populations. In addition, they suggest that Arctic nations, tribal governments, and aboriginal groups should work together by monitoring the harvests of Arctic marine mammals and by collecting genetic samples in remote areas.

There are some very good examples of how the last recommendation might work. One that stands out is Karen Dunmall's attempts at tracking Pacific salmon moving into the Arctic. She offers aboriginal fishermen in the Mackenzie River watershed a reward for reporting and turning in salmon catches. In an effort to spread the word, she has her own website and a Facebook posting that has garnered a lot of "likes" from northerners.

Although the catches Dunmall records do not reflect the true number of salmon entering the Mackenzie River watershed, they at least give scientists the idea of where the salmon are going, whether they might be spawning and how they might affect native species such as Dolly Varden trout, Arctic char, and lake trout.

Had she not been keeping these records, scientists may have not have learned the remarkable story of aboriginal fisherman catching three chum salmon in Great Bear Lake in 2013. Dunmall and Canada Fisheries and Oceans scientist Jim Reist aren't particularly concerned that Pacific salmon will someday compete with the lake's famous trout. Adult chum salmon make their way upstream in the fall before spawning and then dying. The juveniles emerge from the gravel the following spring and head directly to the ocean that same spring or summer. The chances of lake trout and chum salmon meeting, says Dunmall, are greatest during spawning.

Competition could occur, however, during spawning if both fish are targeting the same type of habitat, particularly if that habitat were in short supply. It would be unusual, but not unheard of, for chum salmon to spawn in a lake. It would also be unusual, but not unheard of, for lake trout to spawn in rivers. Stranger things have happened. This story seems to have parallels to the Canada goose–cackling goose interactions.

That said, there is a concern that colonizing chum and pink salmon could interact with other substrate-spawning salmonids such as Dolly Varden trout that dig redds and similarly target areas of groundwater.

In the big picture of things that are shaping the future Arctic, hybridization remains a "what-if" scenario, currently with no clear answers. As opposed to what's currently happening to Pacific walrus off the coast of Alaska and Chukotka, for example, the possibility of genes flowing between Pacific walrus and Atlantic walrus seems minor, especially compared to what is happening to them as ice retreats in that region. Admittedly, hybridization is likely to be a slow process compared with other threats from climate change, but it throws an interesting wrinkle into the question of what species will survive and how, as well as what contributions new species might make to the ecosystem dynamics of the future Arctic.

"Slow," of course, is a risky way of describing what may come of this process in an Arctic world in which scientists are constantly underestimating the pace at which change is taking place.

The polar bear/grizzly bear hybrid is a case in point. It turns out that the polar/grizzly hybrid killed in 2006 was not, as some scientists initially thought, an anomaly. A year before my arrival on Banks Island in 2011, an Inuit hunter had shot another hybrid off the coast of Victoria Island. The following year, biologists Jodie Pongracz and Evan Richardson documented an unprecedented cluster of hybrids and grizzly bears in Viscount Melville Sound northeast of Banks Island where polar bear numbers are sparse and where a grizzly has only been seen once. These sightings of three grizzly and two hybrid bears in close proximity to one another so far north was unprecedented. It could, however, herald even greater changes to come.

Chapter 6

Lords of the Arctic No More

I T WAS MIDNIGHT on the west coast of Hudson Bay where the
Hayes River spills its freshwater into the salty sea. The brisk August wind that had blown hard for most of the day had calmed
down. Inside the one-room cabin I was sleeping in, the glow from a
quickly fading fire in the wood stove flickered. After a full day of being cramped in the backseat of a helicopter counting dozens of polar
bears along the shoreline, I was dead tired and should have been fast
asleep, but the rustling of some creature beneath the plywood floor
was keeping me awake. So was the mystery behind the bloody head of
a polar bear that was tucked under my bunk.

There were three other people in the cabin that night: helicopter
pilot Justin Seniuk, biologist Vicki Trim, and Darryl Hedman, the
regional wildlife manager for the Manitoba government, which is ultimately responsible for polar bears when they are on land here along
the coast from July to late November and sometimes later. Although
it had been more than four months since I had last seen these three
on a late-winter polar bear denning survey, it seemed as if it were just
yesterday. Thankfully, it was about 50 degrees Fahrenheit warmer than
it was back in March, when Seniuk had to stay up all night to keep the
helicopter's engine warm with a generator that kept sputtering out.

Once again, I was sleeping in one of the two lower bunks. Trim was in the bed above me, and the head of the polar bear was below, wrapped up tightly in a green garbage bag. At least we thought it was the head of a polar bear. Neither Trim nor Hedman was completely convinced.

The discovery came earlier in the day when we homed in on a polar bear feeding on the freshly killed carcass of another bear. The scene was puzzling from the beginning, for two main reasons.

Cannibalism among polar bears is extremely rare in cases that do not involve male bears killing juveniles or cubs. The dead animal was not a cub. On those rare occasions when cannibalism does occur, it's usually because one or both of the animals are near the point of starvation. From the air, it was hard to gauge the condition of these two animals.

What really took us aback, though, was what we saw after we chased the cannibal away and then landed. Although the dead bear had the webbed feet, short claws, and elongated skull that are all typical of a polar bear, it looked a little like a grizzly. Its fur was brown, and the snout didn't have the Roman nose that you see on the head of the great white wanderer.

"Jesus Christ, I don't know what to make of this," Hedman said as he ran his fingers through the fur of the animal. "Right off the top, I'd say that this has to be a polar bear. I've seen only one grizzly in all the time I've been doing this, but that was hundreds of miles up the coast. If this is a grizzly, or a grolar [polar/grizzly hybrid], and it could well be, then we may be looking at a new chapter in the natural history of this region."

With that, Hedman walked over to the helicopter to get an axe, which he used to chop off the head of the dead animal. "This is the only way we're going to know for sure what we have here," he said as he swung and planted the blade firmly into its thick neck. "We'll let the experts solve the mystery when we go back south."

As it turned out, the animal was indeed a polar bear, not a grizzly bear/polar bear cross like the ones that have been seen and shot in the western Arctic. This act of cannibalism, as well as several others that have been documented in recent years, was a reminder, however, that polar bears will be the losers in a world in which grizzly bears are expanding their footprint in a warmer Arctic.

Not only are polar bears competing with and sometimes mating with grizzly bears that are encroaching on their territory, they are dealing with the rapid retreat of sea ice that makes it increasingly difficult for them to hunt seals, which represent 95 percent of their diet. Unaccustomed as they are to preying on caribou, ground squirrels, and other tundra animals as the grizzly bear does, the polar bear isn't likely to make up for the shortfall of energy it needs to get it through the summer by eating berries, goose eggs, and the carrion it comes across. The animal is a specialist. Everything about it is finely tuned to the art of killing seals on and along the sea ice edges.

The effect of these changes is showing up in the numbers. Currently, 20,000 to 25,000 polar bears make up nineteen subpopulations in Alaska, Canada, Greenland, Norway, and Russia. According to the International Union for the Conservation of Nature's Polar Bear Specialist Group, only one of these subpopulations was increasing when the group issued its status report in 2014. Five were stable, four were declining, and there was insufficient data to provide an assessment of current trends for the remaining populations.

The bears of western Hudson Bay are among the most vulnerable. Between 1987 and 2004, that population dropped 22 percent. So has denning in the core areas. What's more, recent studies suggest that there are now fewer family groups and fewer bears living beyond their first year of life. Anecdotal reports also suggest that acts of cannibalism such as the one we saw are on the rise.

A similar trend is developing in the western Arctic where scientists are seeing more and more polar bears denning on land rather than on sea ice and more polar bears swimming long distances and sometimes drowning. In the southern Beaufort Sea region, they are also seeing fewer cubs survive longer than six months. The latest estimates suggest that the populations have dropped by at least 25 percent and perhaps by as much as 50 percent.

Ian Stirling has been studying polar bears for more than forty years. He doesn't think that it's going to get any better for polar bears at the southern end of their range. More often than not, the animals he and his colleagues see in these regions are younger, shorter, and thinner than the typical bear seen twenty or thirty years ago. The reason is simple. Bears pile on the fat they need to make it through the year by catching seals on the ice. With the ice now breaking up an average of three weeks earlier in spring as is now the case in western and southern Hudson Bay, the animals are spending more time on land and getting less opportunity to put on the reserves they need to successfully reproduce and for their cubs to make it through the year. It's a double-edged sword. Less time feeding also means more time burning up stored fat. Once that fat burns up, some bears go into town looking for something to eat. The one- or two-week delay in the freeze-up only enhances the chances of polar bears getting into trouble.

Stirling is not alone in thinking that the future Arctic will not be kind to polar bears. He and biologist Steve Amstrup were among the lead authors of a landmark U.S. Geological Survey (USGS) report in 2008 that predicted that two-thirds of world's polar bears, including those in western and southern Hudson Bay and those along the coast of Alaska and the western Arctic of Canada, will disappear by midcentury if sea ice continues to retreat as forecast. By the end of this century, they warned, the only polar bears left will be living in the High Arctic of Canada and Greenland where there may be enough ice and seals around to sustain them.

If the past tells us anything about the future of this species, it's that the current situation may not be as hopeless as it currently looks, even though little or no progress is being made on curbing the greenhouse gas emissions that are warming the Arctic and melting sea ice at an unprecedented rate. Polar bears have been in deep trouble before, and in each case, public policy has saved them.

In the 1960s, for example, better rifles, self-killing guns, the commercialization of the snowmobile, and the shooting of bears from planes and ships fundamentally changed humankind's relationship with the polar bear: the classic confrontation between man and beast turned into an arcade shooting game. Hunters in Alaska were killing so many bears that as many as thirty bush planes were lining up on the ice outside Kotzebue waiting to take trophy hunters out onto the sea ice.

The increase in killings was worldwide. In the 1920s, hunters were slaughtering as many as nine hundred bears annually in Svalbard, the Norwegian archipelago. In one notable case in 1926, an American girl shot eleven bears—six of them in one day—from the deck of Roald Amundsen's old supply ship, *Hobby*.

Polar bear killings in Svalbard did eventually drop off to about five hundred animals annually by the end of World War II, but only because there were so few polar bears left to kill.

The fate of polar bears became so precarious by the early 1960s that Canadian scientist Richard Harington estimated there might be only ten thousand bears left, less than half the population today. No one really knew, but Soviet scientists, who successfully lobbied to get protected status for the polar bear in 1956, thought that Harington was being optimistic. They figured that it was half that number.

The alarms, which were echoed in newspapers such as the *New York Times*, led to the first circumpolar meeting on polar bear conservation in Fairbanks, Alaska. Fortunately for the scientists attending that meeting in 1965, there was genuine political interest in doing something to prevent the bear's extinction. Secretary of the Interior Stewart Udall, Alaska Senator E. L. Bartlett, and Alaska Governor William A. Egan showed up and added their voice to those who were calling for drastic protection measures.

For his part, Bartlett was determined "not to see the polar bear follow the buffalo into extinction."

As Bartlett told delegates at the meeting, "If, as some people fear, the polar bear is in danger of becoming extinct, the world will be less for the loss. . . . If man can still take the time to see and understand the dignity and magnificence and uniqueness of polar bears, there is a good chance that man will meet and pass the necessary moral test."

What followed was extraordinary, considering the Cold War mentality that prevailed at the time. At the conclusion of the meeting, a resolution was passed calling for the protection of denning females and their cubs, which were being shot back then. The United States, Canada, Denmark, Norway, and the Soviet Union—together under the auspices of the International Union for the Conservation of Nature—agreed to pool their resources and research efforts to ensure a future for the species. To that end, they signed a treaty in 1973 that put restrictions on recreational and commercial hunting, banned the hunting of polar bears from aircraft and ships, and made commitments to further research.

By this time as well, the United States had regulated hunting. Norway banned it completely, and the Canadian government limited the

Inuit and the sports hunt to a quota system. In relatively short order, a crisis was averted. Virtually every one of the polar bear subpopulations that was in trouble bounced back. It took a long time—thirty years in some parts of Svalbard—however.

Stirling continues to look back on that period of crisis with amazement.

"For many years, the conservation of polar bears was the only subject in the entire Arctic that nations from both sides of the Iron Curtain could agree upon sufficiently to sign an agreement," he said. "Such was the intensity of human fascination with this magnificent predator, the only marine bear."

That was then, of course, and this is now. Now, the main threat to polar bears is climate change, not hunting or reckless human behavior. Now we have people like Al Gore and organizations such as the World Wildlife Fund and Polar Bears International calling for action, but with some notable exceptions, they have not been as politically effective in getting something done as E. L. Bartlett or Stewart Udall were.

Curbing greenhouse gas emissions is the obvious answer to the problem, but even if that monumental challenge were to be accomplished in the coming years, it would not likely reverse the retreat of Arctic ice for many centuries to come (Figure 6.1). As climate change experts often remind us, one can't simply turn off the switch and expect that global temperatures will stop rising immediately, let alone be reversed in a short time. The effect of a rapidly warming world will continue, perhaps for generations.

Polar bear scientist Andrew Derocher spent seven years researching polar bears in Svalbard for the Norwegian Polar Institute before returning to Canada. He had been thinking about how to manage polar bears in a warming world since the USGS made its dire predictions. Ways needed to be found to give polar bears the extra time they will need to survive until rising global temperature can be brought under control, he thought.

Initially, Derocher got a lot of sympathy, but no serious traction, from his colleagues when he began floating some management options. For some scientists, it did not seem that urgent. Then, in 2010, Péter Molnár, Derocher's graduate student and now a scientist at

Figure 6.1 With sea ice retreating rapidly, polar bears have less time to hunt seals, which represent 95 percent of their diet. Photo credit: Edward Struzik

University of Toronto, turned heads with a mathematical model that suggested that the collapse of some polar bear populations, such as the one in western Hudson Bay, might occur sooner and more catastrophically than the climate models predict.

The Molnár model is predicated on the amounts of energy a polar bear uses to find a mate, produce and nurse cubs, and get by for several weeks—in some cases, several months—when there is no platform of ice from which to hunt seals, their main source of food.

The model was designed to predict what will happen as sea ice recedes and leaves bears with less time to the put on the fat they need. The results were startling. The model suggested that the expected changes in reproduction and survival are not linear, as one might expect, with the population gradually thinning out. Instead, polar bears will likely continue to reproduce, as they are doing now, until they reach a threshold. Once that threshold is passed, reproduction and survival could decline dramatically. In short order, the population will collapse.

Molnár's model lent an air of urgency to the situation once it was published. In the summer of 2012, on the eve of that record-breaking season for ice retreat in the Arctic, twelve polar bear scientists agreed to meet informally at the International Association for Bear Research and Management conference in Ottawa to discuss the management plan idea that Derocher had informally floated a few years before. Not everyone was on the same page, but there was enough common ground to allow Amy Cutting from the Oregon Zoo to produce a list of the various points that were raised. Derocher followed up on Cutting's list with a draft that led to an article in *Conservation Letters*.

In that journal article, he and the others suggested that the day might soon come when some polar bear populations will have to be fed by humans to keep them alive during an extended ice-free season or to prevent them from roaming into small northern communities where they would pose a danger to people and property.

Some bears, they suggested, may have to be placed in temporary holding compounds until it is cold enough for them to go back onto the sea ice. In worst-case scenarios, they envisioned polar bears from southern regions being relocated to more northerly climes that have sufficient sea ice cover. Failing that, those animals that have little chance of being rehabilitated or relocated may have to euthanized. One way or another, they concluded, zoos, which are currently having a tough time getting polar bears because of stiff regulations that prevent them from doing so, are likely going be offered as many animals as they can handle.

Not surprisingly, climate change deniers and sceptics had a field day when newspaper, magazine, and television reporters from all over the world picked up on the story. The fallout, however, did not end there. Inuit leaders, many of whom doubt that polar bears are in trouble, vowed to stop anyone who tried to act on the recommendations. Others scoffed at the cost, estimated to be as much as $32,000 a day, or $1 million a month, to feed the one thousand bears that live along the west coast of Hudson Bay, for example.

Derocher didn't back off.

"If you talk to any of the polar bear biologists, you'll find from them that the public is already asking us about the issues we covered in the paper," Derocher told me days after the article was published. "I've had well-positioned conservation types waiting to start the fund-raising to feed polar bears. In their opinion, lack of progress on greenhouse gases means we will be dealing with crises. I don't view the options we lay out as a way of not dealing with greenhouse gases because without action on that front, there's little that could be done in the longer term to save the species, and we'll see massive range contractions and possibly extinction."

In the world of polar bear science, Derocher has become a worthy successor to Ian Stirling, his thesis supervisor. Derocher pulls no punches in criticizing governments for not doing enough to protect polar bears. Something, he says, needs to be done sooner rather than later, and governments have to be behind it.

"The idea of supplemental and diversionary feeding is nothing new," he says, responding to those who think the ideas are crazy. "It is done for a huge variety of species—from elk in the United States to brown bears in Eastern Europe. It can work if done properly."

Derocher acknowledges that such a solution can be a tough sell to decision makers.

"Keeping hundreds of semiwild bears on a diet of bear chow doesn't fit my personal philosophy," he said. "But perhaps centuries from now, it will be viewed as visionary if we eventually control those greenhouse gases."

Since he retired from the USGS, Steve Amstrup has been senior scientist for Polar Bears International, a group that describes itself as the world's leading polar bear conservation organization. Amstrup emphasizes that the purpose of that article he put his name to was not to promote one management strategy over another or to suggest that they will all work.

"The purpose is to remind the readers, and hopefully policy people, that the long-term future of polar bears is in jeopardy," he told me when I flew with him along the west coast of Hudson Bay one recent autumn day. Amstrup was following up on a report of a dead polar bear on the coastline. The article's second purpose, he explained, was to point out "that the combination of a long-term human caused trend and shorter-term natural climate fluctuations will likely cause some catastrophic loss events long before the long-term trend alone results in reaching too low sea ice thresholds. Third, it makes managers and policy people aware of the various kinds of on-the-ground actions that may be applied to manage these early events and makes them begin to think of the varying levels of cost that may be involved in the different options they may choose."

Amstrup sees some similarities in this call for action to the crisis that polar bear conservation faced in the 1960s, but he believes that there is a difference to account for.

"We really never have been here before," he said. "Yes, before the International Polar Bear Agreement that was signed forty years ago, many scientists were concerned about their future. But the identified threats back then were hunting, mainly, and perhaps industrial development and other on-the-ground activities occurring in polar bear habitat.

"The chief problem now is climate change, which is rapidly melting sea ice. Without sea ice for three to five months a year, many bears will not be able to use it as a feeding platform to hunt their favored prey, ringed seals. As a consequence, polar bears will be forced to spend more time fasting on land, where they pose a greater risk to human populations in the Arctic."

Amstrup realizes that what he and his colleagues are recommending is going to be difficult to sell to policy makers who are now sorely divided on the issue of climate change on ideological grounds. Each strategy will require logistical, financial, and political efforts, not to mention the courage to stare down and convince skeptics that each step is necessary. It may well end up with a worst-case scenario where the primary goal is to preserve the genetic structure of the species in zoos.

He refuses to give up hope, however, in part because he has been in this situation before and has succeeded. No one, for example, thought that the administration of President George W. Bush could be persuaded to list the polar bear as a threatened species, as the administration did shortly after the USGS report was made public in 2008.

Looking back on it now, Amstrup does admit that he was a little surprised by the response to the report. The Bush administration had the Safari Club, the energy industry, the right-wing Science and Public Policy Institute, and many other wealthy organizations urging it not list the polar bear as threatened. The Alaska state legislature was so opposed to this listing that it allocated $2 million in research funding to stop it. The goal was so transparent that *Anchorage Daily News* correspondent Tom Kizzia quipped that the Alaska legislature is "looking to hire a few good polar bear scientists. The conclusions have already been agreed upon—researchers just have to fill in the science part."

The debate, however, took a sharp turn in favor of listing the polar bear in 2005 when the U.S.-based Center for Biological Diversity put together a scientific petition calling for the bear's protection under the Endangered Species Act. Initially, the Bush administration resisted. Center lawyers, however, were tenacious. With partners, they filed twice to compel the government to respond to their petition.

Even then, most everyone thought that the administration would find a way of ignoring the report that Amstrup and his colleagues at the U.S. Geological Survey were commissioned to produce. Rather than dismissing the report when it was handed over to him, however, Secretary of the Interior Dirk Kempthorne reluctantly accepted its recommendations, recognizing perhaps that he had no choice.

"My hope is that the projections from these models are wrong, and that sea ice does not recede further," Kempthorne said a few days later in announcing his decision to list the polar bears as a "threatened" species. "But the best science available to me currently says that this is not likely to happen in the next 45 years."

What followed was not perfect by any stretch of the imagination. The Bush-era mentality that robbed polar bears of protection is gone, though, and 128 million acres of polar bear habitat were set aside in 2009. What is more, American hunters can no longer go to Canada and bring back any part of a polar bear that they kill.

As heartening as these changes are, efforts to protect the polar bear in Canada have not gone nearly as well in recent years. The troubles there began in 2007 when many scientists believed that climate change in the Arctic had reached the tipping point, when winter's freeze could no longer keep up with the summer melt. The heat experienced in 2007 affected everything from glacial runoff to sea ice thinning, the habitat of pikas to polar bears, the Arctic fishery in Alaska, and the distribution of arctic cod in Hudson Bay. For the third year in a row, hundreds of Arctic whales made the mistake of staying in the

Canadian Arctic longer than they should have. The cold snap, which should have taken hold much earlier, trapped one group of more than six hundred narwhals in small pools of open water that closed in so quickly that baby whales were thrown out onto the sea ice by the force of so many adult whales rising up in clumps, gasping for air.

At the time, the status of the polar bear in Canada was up for review by the Committee on the Status of Endangered Wildlife in Canada (COSEWIC) that same year. COSEWIC is an independent committee of wildlife experts and scientists whose main job is to advise government in identifying which species require special attention. Its reports often determine whether an animal, such as the polar bear, is listed as extinct, endangered, threatened, or worthy of special concern, which, ironically, requires no action for recovery.

Most everyone had expected COSEWIC to recommend that the polar bear be listed as "threatened" in light of the rapid retreat of sea ice. Instead, it recommended that that the status of the polar bear remain the same as it was in 1991, a species of "special concern."

Many people were surprised. Derocher, Stirling, and virtually every member of the International Union on the Conservation of Nature's polar bear specialist group, however, were not. One of the coauthors of the report that was done for COSEWIC was well known to them. Mitch Taylor was for a time the polar bear biologist for the territory of Nunavut. Taylor was then, and still is, a climate change sceptic. He pretty much affirmed that position by signing the Manhattan Declaration, which stated in 2008 that combating climate change is "a dangerous misallocation of intellectual capital and resources that should be dedicated to solving humanity's real and serious problems." Signatories like him claimed that "there is no convincing evidence that CO_2 emissions from modern industrial activity [have] in the past, [are] now, or will in the future cause catastrophic climate change."

Taylor was so dead set against what the Bush administration was being petitioned to do to protect the polar bears in 2006 that he wrote a twelve-page letter to the U.S. Fish and Wildlife Service claiming that climate change is not pushing the animals to the brink of extinction. "No evidence exists that suggests that both bears and the conservation systems that regulate them will not adapt and respond to the new conditions," he argued. Warmer temperatures, he went as far as to claim, could increase food sources for polar bears. He also stated that there is no evidence that oil and gas developments and the spread of contaminants in the Arctic will harm the species.

Given all that Taylor had said and done, the top scientists at COSEWIC could have reevaluated his report and recommendations before sending them to the government for consideration. Instead, they rallied round him, insisting that there was nothing wrong with the scientific data that he used to come to his conclusions. One COSEWIC scientist suggested that criticisms from Stirling and Derocher were personal, not professional.

It was all that the Canadian government could hope for. Like George W. Bush, Prime Minister Stephen Harper was, and still is, ideologically opposed to doing anything about global warming. Harper had described the Kyoto Protocol as a "job-killing, economy destroying" accord that was based on "tentative and contradictory evidence about climate trends." Implementing Kyoto, he once said, "would cripple the oil industry."

Under the Harper government, polar bear science has suffered badly. Stirling, who retired from his position as polar bear scientist for Environment Canada, is now an adjunct professor at the University of Alberta, where he is free to say what he wants. Like most government scientists, his successor, Nick Lunn, is not allowed to speak publicly. Lunn's budget for polar bear research has also been cut to the point where he has barely enough helicopter time to monitor polar bears on the west coast of Hudson Bay.

In the meantime, Canada has pretty much abandoned polar bears in the western Arctic, leaving it up to the U.S. Fish and Wildlife Service to account for populations that both countries share in that region. Ironically, through the Bureau of Ocean Energy Management, U.S. government officials have been funding Derocher to do much of that work on the Canadian side.

In the latest development, the Canadian government successfully opposed a U.S. proposal to add the polar bear to the Appendix 1 listing under the Convention on International Trade in Endangered Species (CITES) of Wild Fauna and Flora. CITES is an international agreement between governments. Its aim is to ensure that international trade in specimens of wild animals and plants does not threaten

their survival. The listing would have banned the trade of parts coming from five hundred polar bears legally killed in Canada each year by
Inuit and by sports hunters.

Not everything is as hopeless as it looks in Canada. For the past
forty years, the government of Manitoba has experimented with a variety of innovative ways of dealing with hundreds of polar bears that
end up wandering into or near the small town of Churchill on the
west coast of Hudson Bay. The plan is not perfect by any means, and
unofficially, it has been a work in progress since it first got started in
1966. Back then, Churchill was little more than a backwater port town
that had been in steady decline since the military began pulling out of
the area two years earlier.

The prospects for the future did not look good for Churchill in
those days. One could walk from one end of the town to the other in
ten or fifteen minutes. Along the way, there was the Eskimo Museum,
the Churchill Hotel, the Hudson Hotel, Chez Gizelle, Bay Motors
Garage, the Masonic Hall, the Hudson Bay store, the Mounties' office, and Sigurdson and Martin's Supermarket, whose owners kindly
carried customers' debts until they had the money to pay. That was
about it for commercial enterprises. The Igloo Theatre had closed
its doors for the last time that summer, as had the Steak House, the
town's only restaurant.

The housing situation was even worse. Many of the homes were
tar-papered, bare-framed shacks with additions that had been slapped
on without any observance to municipal codes. Water was trucked in
and stored in fuel drums. Heat came from oil, coal, or wood stoves,
many of which would never have met current safety standards.

According to a government consultant who was sent up to
Churchill to evaluate the living conditions in the late 1960s, health
hazards had been underscored many times before he arrived on the
scene. He blamed the federal government for not preventing the "unparalleled squalor" that existed in the community. Living conditions in
Churchill, he reported, were "among the most wretched in Canada."

The report fell on deaf ears. Instead of offering aid, the Canadian
government announced that 250 people were going to lose their jobs
at the Rocket Range in Churchill that was set up in 1958 to probe
the auroral zone. The northern federal services being offered out of

Churchill were going to be moved to Frobisher Bay (now Iqaluit). Rumors and newspaper editorials followed suggesting that the money-losing port may, or should, be closed. Gordon Beard, the politician representing the region, was so distraught by all the talk that he suggested that the government should "lock the whole show up and leave Churchill to the polar bears."

Polar bears, however, represented another serious problem for Churchillians. After the military pulled out in 1965, more and more of the animals began venturing into town looking for food in one of the community's dumps or, in some cases, peoples' homes. In an effort to protect people and property, as many as twenty-nine bears were being killed each year.

By the early 1970s, it was apparent to all that if nothing were done to address the problem, this situation was going to become a lot worse before it got any better. Remarkably, science, sanity, and public opinion turned things around. When every adult in Churchill was asked in 1976 what could be done to solve the polar bear problem, there were those who predictably suggested that all the animals should be killed. To the surprise of the wildlife specialist who put a copy of the survey in every mailbox, however, a significant number of people desperately wanted to find a way to live with the animals.

Many of the letters were not short, simple responses from ordinary people who, for the most part, led unextraordinary lives, but instead were long, thoughtful reflections on what had happened in the past and what needed to be done in the future. One elderly lady who had experienced more than her share of troubles with polar bears sent in a handwritten note that was four pages long. She apologized for being so verbose. The wildlife specialist was so impressed with the quality of her insights that he asked her to be a member of the committee set up to devise a plan to solve the polar bear problem.

From a public policy perspective, the makeup of the committee was perhaps the single most important reason that the management plan that members came up with was taken seriously. The committee could have been filled with local politicians and government bureaucrats, as is often the case in such situations. Instead, men, women, a trapper, and one aboriginal leader from the community were invited to join the wildlife specialist and a conservation officer on the committee.

Like the twelve scientists who got together in Ottawa in 2012 to discuss management options for polar bears, not everyone in this case was on the same page. There was enough goodwill and sufficient compromising to get the job done, though.

The plan that the Churchill Polar Bear Committee penned in 1977 was visionary. It resulted in what amounted to a polar bear jail for so-called problem bears that would otherwise be shot (Figure 6.2). A more humane protocol for deterring bears was also recommended, and opportunities for wildlife viewing were envisioned. The committee insisted that scientific research and public education needed to guide future management decisions. In short, committee members wanted people to regard the polar bear not as a great white rat that ate garbage, but as a majestic animal that deserved respect.

Most people in Churchill have since learned to love polar bears because the bears in a way saved their town. By 1984, the polar bears of Churchill were such a hot tourist attraction and a cash cow for the town's businessmen that *National Geographic*, *Audubon*, *Smithsonian*, *New York Times*, *Time*, *London's Daily Mirror*, and *La Figaro* had all already devoted considerable space to the subject in magazines and documentaries. In 1984, the editors of *Life* sandwiched a five-thousand-word article about Churchill's polar bears in between one on the Shroud of Turin and another on the twentieth anniversary of the Beatles coming to the United States.

Pierce Roberts, the Manitoba government director who is now responsible for the Polar Bear Alert Program, says that educating people is another reason that the program been so successful. In 2012, not a single animal was killed by the department. In addition, no one has been killed by a polar bear in Churchill since 1983.

Roberts and his team of conservation officers are well aware of the challenges that Derocher and his colleagues outline in their paper. One might have expected, for example, that the 22 percent population decline in polar bears that occurred in western Hudson Bay between 1987 and 2004 would have resulted in a similar reduction in the numbers of problem polar bears coming into Churchill, but the number of problem bear occurrences has actually been rising dramatically. Between 1992 and 2002, officers responded to a total of 1,495 calls. In the decade that followed, that number nearly doubled, to 2,807.

Figure 6.2 Instead of shooting problem bears in Churchill, wildlife officers place the animals in a holding cell for two or three weeks or until the ice has formed on Hudson Bay. Photo credit: Edward Struzik

The added work has been a strain on resources. In 2011, labor costs were four times what they were in 2000, while operating costs doubled in the same period.

"The one thing that we've learned from the past is that there is always going to be a new challenge protecting both people and polar bears in Churchill," says Roberts. "So we have to continue to come up with new ways of dealing with these emerging situations. It's not going to be easy, especially if climate change does what everyone seems to think it's going to do."

Derocher doubts that many of the smaller Inuit communities in the Arctic can afford the resources that the town of Churchill has available to it. He says, though, that one important lesson to come out of the Churchill experience is that all interested parties need to be consulted.

"Polar bears are of extremely high priority for northern communities, but that doesn't negate the fact that they are viewed as a species of global significance by people that live far from polar bear habitat," says Derocher. "The sooner we consider the options, the sooner we'll have a plan. The worst-case scenario is a catastrophically early breakup with hundreds of starving bears followed by inappropriate management actions.

"It has always seemed that we've been behind the curve on the climate change and polar bear file," he adds. "I think this stems from the three-generation perspective on conservation planning—thirty-six to forty-five years for polar bears. That time frame leads one to think you've got time. But the science is clear that this is a fallacy."

This fallacy of short-term thinking is being driven home by the changes that have taken place in western Hudson Bay over the past decade. Ten years ago, wildlife managers like Daryll Hedman scoffed at reports of grizzly bears moving into the area. The last time anyone had seen a grizzly in Manitoba was in 1923, and the bear that was shot in that case was nowhere near the coast. This thinking began to change in 2008, however, when Hedman himself saw one near Churchill. The list of grizzly bear sightings that followed included one in which Pierce Roberts and his boss saw a grizzly eating a polar bear it had killed.

Killer whales have also moved into the kingdom of the polar bear in western Hudson Bay. Scientist Steve Ferguson was just as skeptical as Hedman was when the Inuit and local tour operators in Churchill first started reporting the presence of orcas several years ago. Those doubts, however, turned to genuine fascination as the number of confirmed sightings in western Hudson Bay and in other parts of the Arctic topped the one hundred mark. Ferguson now believes that it's possible that the killer whale could replace the polar bear as the top predator in the marine food chain in western Hudson Bay, if not in the entire Arctic.

Without polar bears, the future Arctic will be a very different place than it is today. Not only will a town like Churchill be impoverished by the loss, but the Inuit who rely on bears for food, clothing, and for the revenue the sports hunt generates will as well.

The polar bear, however, is more than just a source of food and material for clothing and for the much-needed revenue that sports hunting brings to the communities. Nanuq, as the animal is called by the Inuit of Canada, is resourceful and such a good hunter of seals that it is a powerful symbol of who the Inuit were and are as a people, both in life and in death. The Inuit aren't as much afraid of the polar bear as they are in awe at how much it was like them: great hunters of seals.

For this and many others reasons, finding ways of saving polar bears is critical. The loss of this species would not only reverberate throughout the Arctic ecosystem, it would signal defeat in dealing with the climate change that humans are driving. There are no easy solutions. Then again, there were no easy solutions in the 1960s when saving the polar bear involved negotiations with the Soviet Union at the height of the Cold War. In the end, science prevailed in convincing decision makers from every corner of the circumpolar world to do what was necessary to save the largest predator on Earth. There's no reason why it can't happen again.

Chapter 7

Caribou at the Crossroads

A FEW HUNDRED MILES northeast of Great Slave Lake in Canada, there's a small hill that represents the divide between water that flows southwest into the Mackenzie River watershed and water that flows northeast into the Arctic Ocean. The longest of the rivers running northeast to the Arctic is the Back. It flows for 500 miles along eighty-three rapids and waterfalls without a single dam, mine, or well site diverting water or carving up the treeless landscape.

In the summer of 1993, I was in the midst of canoeing from Great Slave Lake to the Arctic Ocean hoping to find the source of the Back River. Hard as I looked from my vantage point on that small hill, I couldn't find the line of whitewater that was supposed to flow northeast from a lake nearby. All I could see in the valley below me was a shallow trickle that flowed intermittently from one tundra pond to another. It seemed as if the long, hot summer we were experiencing had dried up the headwaters of this river.

It had been a tough trip, and I was not relishing the idea of having to tell my three companions that we had many more miles of portaging ahead of us to get to the next big lake that spills into the Back.

Before they could catch up to me at the top of the hill, however, something moving toward me caught my attention. Looking through my binoculars, I could see the silhouette of two caribou in the distance. The animals looked at me and then back again, as if something were driving them forward. At first, I thought that the wolves we had seen earlier in the day were the cause of their concern, but when the two caribou were followed by ten, then dozens, and eventually hundreds more, I realized that I was wrong. We were about to be stampeded.

For three hours, the animals kept coming, clacking and grunting and churning up a cloud of dust that scattered light from the setting sun into a blaze of fiery oranges and reds. It was mesmerizing. In all the years I had been hiking, canoeing, and participating in various wildlife surveys in the Arctic, I had never seen so many animals on the move. Ten thousand? Fifteen thousand? Thirty thousand? Confronted by so many caribou marching across such a vast space over a short period of time, it was futile to think that any of our estimates were remotely close to being accurate.

There are several types of wild caribou and reindeer in the world: those that live relatively sedentary lives in the boreal forest, those that spend much of their time in the mountains, those like the Svalbard reindeer and Peary caribou that live year-round in the High Arctic, and those like the Bathurst herd we saw that day that migrate long distances across the barren-ground tundra before retreating to the shelter of the treeline in early autumn and staying there for most of the winter.

Barren-ground caribou are most impressive for their epic migrations across mountains, tundra, deep snow, and freezing rivers and for the extraordinary number of animals that make up individual herds. Keeping an account of them is expensive, difficult, and dangerous. In late June and July when insect harassment compels caribou to bunch up, biologists and technicians fly over in fixed-wing airplanes equipped with aerial cameras mounted on the bellies of the planes. Previously radio-collared animals help the pilots home in on the biggest groups.

Depending on the size of the herd, it can take up to three days of flybys to count or photograph a sufficient number of animals to produce a census. More often than not, weather complicates the survey. Also, herds can overlap in some places. The real work, however, begins after the flights, when biologists sit in dark offices and count the number of animals on photographs projected onto a wall.

In 1986, scientists were reasonably confident that there were more than 450,000 animals in the Bathurst caribou herd. More than twice the size of the Porcupine caribou herd, which inhabits Alaska and the Yukon and Northwest Territories, these animals never got the attention the Porcupine herd received when energy companies launched a determined campaign in the 1980s to open up the calving grounds in the Arctic National Wildlife Refuge in Alaska to development. Without roads, mines, or well sites in the central Arctic to be concerned about, no one suspected the Bathurst herd was in peril.

In the 1.6 million years that caribou have roamed the northern hemisphere, their populations have risen and fallen with cycles of glaciation and deglaciation. In that time, caribou found a way to survive when many other Ice Age animals such as the woolly mammoth didn't. In more recent millennia, populations have ebbed and flowed on a regional basis for a variety of other reasons, not all of them clearly understood. So when the Bathurst herd began showing signs of decline around the time I was on that canoe trip, no one was overly concerned. A few eyebrows were raised in 2003, however, when only a third of these animals could be accounted for. Still, there was no panic. That didn't set in until 2009 when the herd plummeted to just 32,000.

This drop precipitated a flurry of meetings, analyses, and workshops to generate a spectrum of management proposals. It was a tough time to be a politician or a caribou biologist in the north when a hunting ban was proposed as the best means of facilitating a recovery. The ban, which went into effect in 2010, was met with legal challenges from aboriginal groups and angry words from sports hunters who couldn't understand how so many animals could disappear in such a short period of time.

The Bathurst herd is not the only population of caribou that is in serious trouble. According to the CircumArctic Rangifer Monitoring and Assessment Network, which is run on a voluntary basis by veteran biologists Don Russell, Anne Gunn, and others, half of the world's twenty-four barren-ground caribou herds that are routinely counted are in decline. Only three, maybe four, are increasing, and they are doing so only modestly. Measured another way by scientists Liv Vors and Mark Boyce who included the fate of boreal forest and mountain caribou in their survey, thirty-four of the forty-three major herds that scientists have studied worldwide in the past decade are in decline, with caribou numbers plunging 57 percent from their historical peaks.

Based on everything that I heard at the North American caribou workshop held in the Yukon in May 2014, many of those declines are just as breathtaking in scope as the recent fall of the Bathurst herd has been. Biologist Julien Mainguy recounted with dismay how in northern Quebec and Labrador there are now no more than 16,000 animals in the George River herd that once exceeded 800,000 in the 1980s. Mike Setterington described how challenging it is going to be to manage iron-ore mine development risks at Mary River on Baffin Island where caribou numbers on the island have declined from 180,000 to 12,000.

The declines, it appears, are circumpolar, somewhat synchronous and all too familiar to the aboriginal leaders who participated in the Yukon workshop that brought together more than 350 experts. "Talk to our elders and they'll tell you of a time not so long ago when entire mountains were moving with caribou," said Sean Smith, a councilor with the Kwanlin Dün First Nation in the Yukon. "It isn't just the food on the table that we miss, it's the ways in which caribou ties us all together as a people."

Caribou are to Inuit, Dene, and other Arctic people what bison were to the North American Indians. When bison were wiped out on the Great Plains, tribal and First Nations cultures collapsed and never fully recovered.

The absence of caribou in a future Arctic would be just as devastating. Four or five caribou can save a family living in a remote village or hamlet between $2,000 and $4,000 annually in food costs. The importance of these animals, however, extends far beyond scales of economy. Visit any community in Alaska, northern Canada, northern Scandinavia, Greenland, or Arctic Russia and you see caribou in the clothes people wear, the stories they write and tell, and the artwork they create. Like the polar bear, the caribou plays a near mythical role in many people's lives. Each time a hunter kills a caribou, an offering is made to God or the Creator.

Overhunting, however, is one reason caribou have declined in some places. Until 2009, the annual aboriginal harvest from the Bathurst herd alone was between 4,000 and 7,000 animals. Many of them were cows, which are key to the sustainability of a herd. According to one study, the number of breeding females in the herd fell from 203,800 in 1986 to just 16,400 in 2009 (Figure 7.1).

Hunting alone does not account for the freefall, though. What concerns many caribou experts now is the precipitous warming in the Arctic that is adding to the stress that caribou already face in a world in which deep snow, predators, pathogens, insects, and overgrazing limit their numbers.

These climate-induced factors include bigger, hotter, and more frequent forest and tundra fires, extreme weather and ice storms, changes in the dates of freeze-up and breakup of large rivers and lakes, which may affect migrations, a new parasitic disease previously unknown in caribou that live in the Great Bear Lake area of the Northwest Territories, and weather conditions favoring insects that torment the animals and prevent them from foraging and gaining the body mass needed to successfully reproduce.

I saw firsthand the suffering that flies and other insects can cause not only to caribou, but to humans as well when we canoed the Back River in 1993. On warm, calm days, the clouds of blackflies were so thick that when walking through them I felt a little like Moses parting the Red Sea. Turning around at any given time, I could see the path I had just taken. Invariably, evening dinners were topped off with a layer of black protein that was not intended to be part of the recipe. And more often than not, the first half hour in the tent at night was spent squashing thousands of flies that had followed us in. Only then did I realize that, in sufficient numbers, a pile of dead blackflies smells a little like rotting fish.

There were days when we saw big bull caribou running up and down the river madly trying to find relief. Occasionally, some of them would throw themselves into the rapids ahead of us without regard for what might be coming their way. On one warm, calm night, about a dozen caribou trampled through our camp, knocking over the canoes and scattering our gear in what must have been a desperate attempt to find relief.

Figure 7.1 Caribou and reindeer numbers have dropped dramatically in the past two decades for a variety of reasons, including overhunting. Photo credit: Edward Struzik

It was clear that these animals would rather run themselves ragged than forage on the lichens and other vegetation they need to help them through long, hard winters when they sometimes have to travel through heavy snow to escape predators. One crude model that caribou biologists came up with several years ago demonstrates, at least in theory, how this combination of insects and snow could affect the fortunes of the Porcupine caribou herd over a ten-year period.

Taking into account predation, hunting, and the physiology of the animal, the model suggests that the population would grow substantially, from 155,000 to nearly 214,500, if insect harassment was low in summer and snow depths were low in winter and autumn. If the snowfall was moderate, however, the population would decline slightly. Heavy snowfall and a high level of insect harassment would drop the numbers to less than 116,000.

As crude as this model is, at least one study in southern Norway has shown that this situation is actually happening in the real world. Rather than increasing foraging times to compensate for harrying by insects, the animals that were being harassed lost body mass.

Another concern is the possibility of rain falling in the Arctic when there is already snow on the ground. Followed by the cycling of thawing and freezing that happens in late spring, the combined effects can be lethal for an animal forced to dig through hard snow and ice to get to the lichens and other vegetation that lie below.

Biologist Frank Miller discovered the effect of rain in the most unexpected way in 1974 when he was assigned the task of counting Peary caribou, a diminutive animal that is found only on the Arctic islands of Canada. Back in 1961, when the first aerial survey of the Arctic islands was done, biologists crudely estimated Peary caribou numbers to be 49,000. Thirteen years later, Miller could find very few of them. Initially, he thought that he might have somehow screwed up the count. Back home, he searched through the meteorological records to see if he could find something in the data to account for what he might have missed. Those records suggested that rain, which had fallen on snow in the fall of 1973, likely made it hard for caribou to crater through to the lichen that lay below. The heavy snow that followed that winter didn't help. What made it lethal, however, was the viscous cycle of thawing and freezing that hardened things up even more in spring.

Miller estimated that 85 percent of the Peary caribou and 70 percent of the musk oxen on the Arctic islands starved to death that year. The population, he believes, had recovered to a degree in the ensuing years before another devastating icing event in 1995–1996 occurred.

This time, Miller was there to see how it had unfolded. Not only did he find emaciated caribou on the ground, he told me when I joined him in the field sometime later, he saw tracks that suggested that both caribou and musk oxen on one island attempted to cross the sea ice to another island that may not have been as severely affected.

Following the tracks of one herd, Miller found a group of musk oxen on the sea ice bunched up in a circle with their heads pointing out, as they do when wolves attack. Curious to see why the animals did not respond to the approach of the helicopter, Miller had the pilot land so that he could get a closer look. Only when he got to within several feet of the animals did he realize that they were all dead, frozen stiff and leaning up against one another like statues. Miller figured that the animals had been on their last legs when they had embarked on their search for food. It was, he said, one of the strangest things he had seen in his three-decade-long career in the Arctic.

Peary caribou in Canada are not the only animals that are vulnerable to this phenomenon of rain on snow. In a study reported in 2013 by Brage Bremset Hansen, a scientist with the Norwegian University of Science and Technology, reindeer as well as rock ptarmigan, sibling vole, and arctic fox are also being affected by these rain-on-snow events.

Although there is evidence to suggest that such events have happened in the past, there are also studies and anecdotal evidence that indicate that they are likely to occur more often in the future. In recent decades, the Arctic has been heating up twice as fast as the rest of the northern hemisphere—with temperatures routinely rising by 3.5 to 5 degrees Celsius—making autumn rains, early spring thaws, and severe icing events increasingly common.

These rising temperatures in spring are also making it more difficult for caribou to exploit food when they need it most. Because spring arrives earlier and earlier, the flush of highly nutritious plant growth has advanced. In some places, though, caribou reproduction and calving are not occurring earlier, meaning that the calves are born past the peak of prime forage availability.

In addition, the lichen and other tundra plants favored by caribou are gradually being replaced by shrubs and trees that are advancing up mountainsides and northward onto the tundra. If forest and tundra fires accelerate along with this shrubification of the Arctic, says Kris Hundertmark of the Institute of Arctic Biology in Alaska, moose should do well. Caribou in northeast North America, however, could lose up to 89 percent of their habitat, he adds, and caribou elsewhere could suffer through a 60 percent loss.

Caribou could well have trouble competing with moose in this changing landscape structure. The biggest threats to caribou, however, may be energy, forestry, and mining developments that are encroaching on and carving up their habitat. We are already seeing changes in the sub-Arctic boreal forests of Canada where roads, pipelines, drilling platforms, mines, dams, and other human developments are shrinking the size and quality of old-growth forests that caribou there favor. Wolves love this kind of fragmentation because it opens up new territory to deer, which are prolific in their ability to reproduce.

In such situations, caribou can move to new territory, adapt, or die. In its latest report in 2011, the Alberta Caribou Committee seems to suggest that caribou are most likely to die. Three of the province's eighteen herds are at immediate risk of disappearing altogether because of habitat loss. Six of the others are in decline, three are stable, and not enough is known about the remaining six to determine how well they are doing. Scientists on the committee are confident, however, that those herds are in decline as well.

The situation is almost as bad in British Columbia, where government biologists are taking the extreme measure of temporarily fencing in caribou to keep them from being so vulnerable to predation. They are following the lead of biologists in the Yukon who between 2003 and 2006 successfully used fencing to protect some females and calves in the Chisana herd, which ranges along the borderlands of western Yukon and eastern Alaska, near the headwaters of the White River in the Nutzotin Mountains.

Alberta is considering building an even bigger fence, one that would enclose caribou in an area that is at least 1,500 square kilometers. So far, though, that idea hasn't gotten beyond the boardrooms of the oil and gas and the forestry companies that would likely bear the costs associated with building and maintaining it.

Biologists Richard Schneider and Stan Boutin suggest that it's time to get into triage mode and give up on some of those herds that are on the brink of extinction. In crunching the numbers relating to the cost of conservation, they and resource economist Vic Adamowicz came up with a scenario that suggests that both government and industry may be better off focusing on relatively undisturbed caribou habitat, such as that found in and around Wood Buffalo National Park and the Alberta/Northwest Territories boundary, than on areas that are already highly fragmented by energy projects.

Protecting just 60 percent of the caribou range, they conclude, could still allow for 98 percent of the energy and forest resource value in Alberta to be maintained. Attempting to save all caribou herds, however, could result in tens of billions of dollars in lost revenues.

"The choice of how many caribou herds to save is a societal one, a job for politicians and land managers, not scientists," Schneider told me. "But the current approach of focusing conservation efforts on the most endangered herds appears to be unwise."

The developments affecting woodland caribou at the southern end of their geographical range are quickly moving north into barren-ground caribou territory.

In the Baker Lake region west of Hudson Bay, French mining giant Areva is proposing to build a $1.5 billion uranium mine near the calving grounds of the Beverly caribou herd. This herd's numbers have fluctuated considerably in recent decades, going from an estimated 210,000 in 1971 to 110,000 in 1980 and then to 286,000 in 1994. Aerial surveys done in the past several years show a steep drop in both the number of cows and the number of calves, indicating that the herd now contains far fewer animals than in the mid-1990s.

At Mary River on northern Baffin Island, Baffinland, the mining company that Mike Setterington has done research for, has plans to build the North American Arctic's largest open-pit mine and transport between 18 million and 20 million metric tons of iron ore along a rail line that it plans to build across 100 miles of tundra.

Fracking—short for hydraulic fracturing—which has caused so much controversy in southern Canada and the United States, is also beginning to have an effect on the Arctic. The fragmentation of caribou habitat that has resulted from shale gas and conventional oil and gas exploration in the Great Bear Lake region of the Northwest Territories is already approaching the thresholds that were outlined in the Government of Canada's boreal caribou recovery strategy.

Across the Arctic, the story is much the same. In the central region of the Russian Arctic, the reindeer-herding Evenks have been struggling to stop a $13 billion hydroelectric development that will flood an area ten times the size of New York City. In Greenland, a 22-mile access road that was built in 2000 between the Kangerlussuaq airport and the Greenland Ice Cap has already caused a major habitat alteration for the Kangerlussuaq-Sisimiut herd. The road provides year-round access for tourists, day-trippers, and hunters, but it traverses what was once sensitive habitat for the herd during the calving and postcalving periods. Now, Alcoa, the world's largest producer of aluminum, wants to build a giant smelter in the region along with several hydro dams to power it.

The news, however, is not all bad. Some of it, in fact, is quite good. After several years in which unfavorable weather made counting the Porcupine caribou herd almost impossible, the survey done in 2012 suggests a total of 197,000 animals, the highest level seen since surveys were first started in 1972. Even though limits on hunting had been put into place, almost no one saw that increase coming.

In Alaska, the Forty Mile herd that disappeared from 90 percent of its range in central Alaska and the Yukon recently crossed the Yukon border for the first time in decades. Where there were only 6,000 animals in 1973, there are now 56,000.

Wildlife managers can do only a handful of things to help facilitate a recovery. They can kill, sterilize, or remove wolves as they routinely did in the past and still do to a lesser extent today. They can ban or restrict hunting as they did with the Bathurst and Forty Mile caribou herds and are attempting to do in Labrador where the George River herd dwells. Or they can ensure that caribou habitat—the calving grounds in particular—are protected from development as the United States and Canada did in the Arctic National Wildlife Refuge, in Ivvavik National Park in the Yukon, and in Tuktut Nogait National Park in the Northwest Territories and Nunavut. When all else fails, they can transplant caribou as they did on Southampton Island at the north end of Hudson Bay in 1968, a decade after the last animal there was killed.

Wolves have long been used as scapegoats for wildlife management problems. For much of the twentieth century, the U.S. and Canadian governments systematically targeted wolves. Initially, wildlife managers used bounties to encourage people to kill wolves. Then they used poison, leghold traps, and marksmen from helicopters to wipe out these predators. In extreme cases, such as in northern Minnesota, men were sent to dig out dens and strangle wolf pups. Even the First Nations of the North had their own form of predator control, killing pups in some cases or removing them from dens and breeding them with their sled dogs.

Sometimes these predator control programs worked too well, as they did in Yellowstone National Park in Wyoming and Banff

National Park in the Canadian Rockies where wolves were completely extirpated. (They have since come back to Banff, albeit in small numbers, and have been successfully reintroduced in Yellowstone.) Most times, though, the programs failed because biologists underestimated just how quickly a wolf population can rebound as long as there is prey for them to exploit.

These heavily criticized wolf eradication programs have been discontinued almost everywhere in North America except in Alberta, British Columbia, and Alaska. The only difference now is that wildlife managers think that they have a better handle on how to make wolf control programs work: according to the formula that most predator control experts rely on, if you kill at least 60 percent—80 percent is preferable—of the wolves in an area, you will begin to see a rebound in prey species after several years as long as there is suitable habitat in which the prey species can recover.

Biologist Bob Hayes has killed 851 wolves and sterilized many others in the name of science and conservation biology. For nearly two decades, he thought that he was doing what needed to be done to protect caribou, moose, and other prey species in the Yukon Territory. Even when protesters chained themselves together in the Yukon legislature, damaged aircraft he was to fly in, followed him to work, and stalked his house, he refused to back away from what he believed.

Years after Hayes retired from government, he was asked by a wildlife management organization whether killing wolves should be considered as a way of stopping the decline of the Porcupine caribou herd, which most everyone thought was in decline at the time. His answer was an emphatic "No." When asked whether there are circumstances in which predator control might be acceptable, Hayes answered in a similar way.

"I spent eighteen years studying the effects of lethal wolf control on prey populations," says Hayes, whose self-published book, *Wolves of the Yukon*, got a lot of attention when it came out in 2010. "The science clearly shows killing wolves is biologically wrong."

Hayes believes that nonlethal ways of controlling wolves may be a better alternative to killing them. He points to the surgical sterilization of fifteen packs that inhabited the summer range of the Forty Mile herd in Alaska. Sterilization and the relocation of 140 other wolves in the area contributed to the recovery of that population.

Although Hayes would rather see wildlife managers leave wolves alone, he offers praise for an innovative plan that Yukon biologists came up with to increase calf survival in the Chisana herd in the Yukon, which had declined from 1,800 animals in 1987 to 700 in 2003. In that case, 115 pregnant cows were captured and transported to a fenced-in enclosure where they were fed reindeer food and hand-picked lichen. Protected against wolves and bears, the cows were released once the calves they gave birth to in the enclosure were old enough to take flight from predation. The enclosures increased the survival rate of the calves from 10 to 75 percent.

In Alberta, where wolves have been systematically poisoned and shot since 2006, government biologists tried and failed to successfully fence in pregnant caribou in 2010. No one knows exactly why it didn't work, but scientists believe that the landscape that the caribou were released into is just too carved up by energy developments to allow them to make a go of it. What they need, they say, is a protected area that is unfragmented by oil and gas and forestry developments (Figure 7.2).

Stan Boutin doesn't disagree. In a study he coauthored with Richard Schneider, he found that there were a total of 34,773 wells, 66,489 kilometers of seismic lines, 11,591 kilometers of pipelines, and 12,283 kilometers of roads that had been built in caribou country in west central and northern Alberta. Not included are the vast areas of forest that have been logged.

Open areas support moose, elk, and especially white-tailed deer and mule deer. As the number of these creatures expands, so does the number of wolves. More often than not, caribou, which rely on old-growth forests for lichen and predator protection, are nothing more than passing targets as wolves move easily from one clear-cut to another through the shrinking old-growth forest.

Offering advice to scientists at the 2014 caribou workshop in the Yukon, Elston Dzus, a biologist who works for Alberta Pacific Forest Industries in northern Alberta, predicted that deer would be, in his words, the "Achilles' heel" of caribou conservation in the Arctic if a way is not found to halt their migration northward. Dzus didn't offer any advice on how that might be done, but the only way of doing it is to hire people to shoot the deer as they cross the border, and the likelihood of that happening is virtually nonexistent if not impossible.

Figure 7.2 Caribou may be more resilient to climate change than many scientists believe. What they need most is space, especially on their calving grounds. Photo credit: Edward Struzik

The ultimate solution is to protect or restore caribou habitat, which the Canadian government promised to do in 2012 in its long-overdue, court-ordered woodland caribou recovery strategy. The plan requires that 65 percent of the habitat that the caribou live in be left undisturbed. In ranges where less than 65 percent of boreal caribou habitat remains undisturbed, the strategy requires that the disturbed habitat be restored to the critical threshold. Even then, local caribou have only a 60 percent chance of being self-sustaining.

Despite this promise and spending millions of dollars on advertising in the *New York Times, Washington Post, New Yorker,* and other media telling the world what a good job Canada is doing environmentally, little has come from these efforts. That point was driven home on the second day of the 2014 caribou workshop when participants learned that the Alberta government had decided to sell off 1,700 hectares of undisturbed caribou habitat that are critical to the recovery of two endangered herds. Once again, the revenue that comes from energy development trumped the costs of caribou conservation.

Arctic governments will inevitably face the same dilemma if oil and gas developments—along with diamond, gold, iron ore, and uranium mines—continue to carve up the tundra. That is not to say that caribou can't survive amid some development. If the iron ore mine at Mary River on Baffin Island goes ahead, it will at least have an adaptive management strategy that Mike Setterington helped devise that will allow mining operators to deal with caribou management issues as they emerge.

Mary River and the three—and soon to be four—diamond mines northeast of Great Slave Lake may not make a big difference to the future of caribou as long as companies do as Baffinland promises. The prospect of dozens and possibly hundreds more developments in the future will, however, especially when heavy snow, extreme weather, icing events, fire, changing vegetation, predators, and insect harassment are factored into future scenarios.

We've seen it happen before. In 1974, there was only one oil sands company operating in Alberta. Almost no one back then, not even the Alberta government, anticipated the tsunami of developments that were coming. Biologist Jan Edmonds, however, sensed an impending disaster for caribou as early as 1979 when she radio-collared and tracked twenty-four caribou that lived in the mountains and foothills of west-central Alberta. I remember it well because I spent a miserable day with her in 1981 bouncing along in the backseat of a fixed-wing airplane searching for the animals, which were already in sharp decline.

Thinking that she was a natural-born optimist, I was surprised when she bluntly told me that these animals were doomed if the government didn't set aside the habitat that they needed. A ban on hunting wouldn't do it, she insisted. The government, though, never listened to her or to the members of the many expert committees that have been set up since then to advise them on caribou management. Time and time again, environmentalist and native groups have used legal action to force the government to take emergency action to protect caribou and other species at risk. In a February 2014 decision, the Federal Court of Canada declared that the Minister of the Environment and the Minister of Fisheries and Oceans acted unlawfully in delaying taking action for several years.

Anne Gunn is very much like Edmonds in voicing her concerns about the whittling away of caribou habitat in the Arctic, especially because it is occurring just as the animals are feeling the effects of global warming. Like paleontologist Grant Zazula, Gunn, who has more than thirty years of field experience, believes that caribou can adapt to these climatic changes. If nothing is done to protect critical caribou habitat, especially the critical calving grounds and migration corridors, however, she doesn't think that they will. Of twenty-four large caribou herds, only the calving grounds of the Porcupine and Bluenose West herds are fully or largely protected.

"For caribou it is all about 'space'—their perceptions of what space they need, including the space needed to distance themselves from us," says Gunn. "Climate change and overhunting are very serious factors that need to be addressed. But unless we give caribou the space they need, I'm afraid we're going to see these declines continue."

In the event that some caribou herds continue to decline to the point where they will be extirpated, there is always the possibility of capturing some and reintroducing them to the wild in the future. This scheme—the final option—has been tried before in places such as Southampton Island at the north end of Hudson Bay in Canada.

Transplants, however, are fraught with political, cultural, and logistical challenges, as wildlife managers in the Northwest Territories discovered in 1997.

In 1997, the year after the second icing event in the High Arctic wiped out 90 percent of the Peary caribou, Gunn and her colleagues came up with a daring plan. The Canadian military would fly a Hercules airplane up to Bathurst Island in the Arctic Archipelago where a wildlife crew was standing by to capture some animals. These caribou would be delivered to a game farm owned by the Calgary Zoo and held there for twenty, fifty, or even a hundred years until the time was ripe to bring them back to the High Arctic.

In some ways, it was a miracle that everyone, including the Canadian military, came on board as quickly as they did to see the plan through. Unfortunately, no one consulted with the Inuit who would be directly affected. So, when the first attempt to airlift the animals was foiled by a blizzard at the last minute, Inuit leaders stepped in and made it known that they were philosophically opposed to the idea of any wild animals being rounded up and placed in a zoo-like enclosure. Faced with the prospects of court action and a nasty public relations battle, the Northwest Territories government backed down.

Unpopular as this idea turned out to be, there is merit in discussing other similar but made-in-the-Arctic options, which are more likely to get local support from Inuit and First Nations than ones that are designed and administered by southerners.

I was reminded of that while flying with Yukon government biologist Tom Jung the day before the 2014 caribou workshop. At the time, Jung wasn't looking for caribou. Instead, he was searching for wood bison that had been reintroduced to the territory 350 years after they had disappeared from the landscape.

Few people were in favor of the reintroduction plan when the first of 142 bison were brought north and then released from a fenced-in site between 1988 and 1992 as part of a national conservation effort to restore wood bison to their former range. It didn't help when none of the animals did what everyone had expected them to do. Instead, three of the animals marched west to Alaska, forcing a conservation officer from Whitehorse to bring them back. The rest moved east into the Ruby Range and Aishihik Lake area east of Kluane National Park. First Nations people didn't want them there because of fears that the bison might displace moose and caribou that were already in danger of disappearing. One ornery bull made matters worse when he knocked down the outhouse of a respected elder. More than a few non-natives saw the transplant as a waste of taxpayer money.

Those negative feelings began to change, however, when the bison numbers rose to levels that allowed for the hunting of the animals. "We restricted hunting to the winter months to give calves a chance to grow and to limit the damage that might be done to the vegetation if hunting were allowed in spring and summer," Jung told me that day. "It's proved to be very popular because bison are the only animal you can hunt in winter in the Yukon. It's given people something to do on the land and to look forward to at that time of year."

Most people, he added, are now comfortable with the idea of bison on the landscape because they are becoming part of the ecosystem.

"After twenty or so years, wolves are now preying on calves. Squirrels are using their hair to build nests. And First Nations, hunters, and local people have a say in how these animals are managed."

Jung has no doubt that wood bison will do well in a future Arctic. "Biologists once thought that wood bison needed forest/wetland landscapes like there are in the Peace-Athabasca delta area in and around Wood Buffalo National Park," he says. "No one considered them to be mountain animals. But once things start greening up in a week or two, most of the bison we see in these valleys below us will start migrating up to the hilltops. I've seen bison looking down at sheep, which is bizarre. The only things that slow them down are deep snow and big frozen lakes. For some reason, they have no interest in walking across ice."

The key to success, Jung figures, is to go slow. "There are no shortcuts in reintroducing animals to a landscape they once inhabited," he says.

Like polar bears in the 1960s, wood bison have been on a fast track to extinction for some time. The animals once inhabited Siberia, Alaska, the Yukon, and the Northwest Territories, but they virtually disappeared during the last few hundred years because of overhunting and climatic changes. By 1900, there were fewer than three hundred animals remaining in a small pocket of wilderness along the Alberta–Northwest Territories border in and around the Peace-Athabasca delta.

Most everyone assumed that the chance to preserve this last pure herd of wood bison was lost when the Canadian government transplanted 6,673 plains bison to the region between 1925 and 1928. Not only did these animals interbreed freely with the wood bison that were already there, they brought with them tuberculosis and brucellosis that they had been infected with while grazing alongside cattle down south.

By sheer chance, a small herd of what appeared to be pure wood bison was spotted from the air in an isolated region of Wood Buffalo National Park in 1957. When Canadian Wildlife Service biologist Nick Novakowski snowmobiled in to have a look, he confirmed that they indeed were wood bison.

In an effort to preserve the genetics of these disease-free animals, eighteen wood bison were transplanted to the newly created

Mackenzie Bison Sanctuary 300 kilometers to the north of Wood Buffalo National Park. Another twenty-one were moved to Elk Island National Park in Alberta, which had been created in 1913 to provide a sanctuary for declining elk populations and for plains bison that had been overhunted to the brink of extinction.

The Canadian national parks service was never really happy about dealing with a fenced-in population of animals that grew by leaps and bounds because there were no predators in the park. To keep the wood bison from eating themselves out of house and home and starving to death, as many did in those first decades, the agency built an abattoir so that the herds could be thinned out. When public pressure forced them to abandon that option, they began looking for people and places that wanted the animals.

In the past, park wardens felt more like farmers than wildlife managers, and many of them made it no secret that they would rather be in another park. From this original population of three hundred wood bison, however, more than four thousand disease-free animals have been returned to the wild in the Northwest Territories, Yukon, and Russia as well as Alaska, which is currently developing a wood bison restoration program.

As disease and habitat destruction takes its toll on wildlife populations across the continent, Parks Canada and those once-reluctant wardens now realize that the wood bison liability they had to live with for so many years has turned into an asset: a wildlife bank that can be dipped into when the opportunity to restore species in former habitat presents itself.

The idea of creating a wildlife bank for barren-ground caribou may be a far-flung one when there are still two million or more in the wild. It could, however, be an insurance policy for preserving the genetics of woodland and mountain caribou, Peary caribou, and Svalbard reindeer, the last of which are barely hanging on in Spitsbergen.

When all is said and done, however, the cheapest and most effective way of ensuring that there will be caribou in a future Arctic is to set aside habitat before industry has a chance to come in, carve it up, and tear it apart. The population of the Porcupine caribou rebounded thanks, in part, to indigenous hunters on all sides of the Alaska, Yukon, and Northwest Territories borders who agreed on hunting restrictions. It's doubtful that this population would have come back had energy companies been successful in their efforts to drill in the Arctic National Wildlife Refuge of Alaska as they have been trying to do. Protection of those calving grounds as well as those in Ivvavik National Park means that there's one less thing stressing these animals.

The past tells us that caribou were more resilient than Ice Age animals such as the woolly mammoth, which was well equipped to deal with the Arctic climate. That's not to say that new anthropogenic stressors are not a threat. There is no denying that caribou are currently losing ground, but it does appear that they are more adaptable than we acknowledge. Unlike the ice that polar bears rely on, caribou habitat is vulnerable to something that we have a bit more control over. Given the space that they need, caribou could and probably will be an important piece of the ecological puzzle in the future Arctic, as long as decision makers set aside the habitat that they need.

Chapter 8

Paradise Lost

THE EARLY SUMMER MORNING got off to a calm start off the west coast of Hudson Bay until a sudden gust of wind began sweeping 6-foot swells in from the open sea. Gazing out at a wall of fog that was slowly heading toward us, biologist Gordon Court started thinking out loud about heading back to the Inuit town of Rankin Inlet.

Once we spotted the telltale excrement of a raptor white-washed on a cliffside, however, Court decided instead to steer the boat toward the nearest landing to get a closer look. Not only was there a peregrine falcon sitting on the ledge of the cliff, it was perched overlooking a nest below.

Peregrines are said to be the fastest birds in the world, capable of catching and killing prey as large as a snow goose. That, however, wasn't what I was thinking about when I headed up the cliff to have a look at the nest while Court went back to the boat to gather the gear he needed to trap and band the bird.

This female, however, had no intention of letting me get anywhere near her nest. Her high-speed stoops started well before I got halfway up the cliff. It was clear that she had every intention of taking off my head before I got any closer. With no easy way of getting back down quickly, it was all I could do to squeeze into a narrow gap in the rock wall before she swooped in for a second try.

Even then, I was not out of harm's way. Screeching with ear-piercing fury, she flew in feet first and exposed her razor-sharp talons within inches of my face. I could see then why John James Audubon called the peregrine the "big footed hawk." If this gal were human, I thought to myself, she'd need size-30 shoes.

If the truth be told, I didn't know what to do at that point except to try to make myself skinny enough to press a little farther back into that crack in the rock wall. That's when I felt a sharp pinch. Too cramped to turn and see what was hurting me, I kept my eye on the dive-bombing falcon. Another pinch followed and then two and then three more. If I hadn't known any better, I would have sworn that there was a young sniper somewhere on the tundra shooting at me with a BB gun.

I could see out of the corner of my eye that Court, down below, was cocking his head from one shoulder to the other, presumably wondering, just as I was, what was causing me to do this dangerous dance on the rock ledge. Then, just as the peregrine was coming in to inflict what I fully expected might be the final, fatal stoop, the nest of angry wasps that I had inadvertently backed into burst into a cloud of buzzing madness.

Fortunately for me, the peregrine aborted her attack long enough for me to clamber back down to the ground.

The next thing I remember, I was on my back huffing, puffing, and rubbing my wounds as Court stood over me smiling. "Good thing these peregrines are not the size of pterodactyls," he quipped. "Otherwise caribou would be in trouble."

Each year, tens of millions of birds migrate to the Arctic and sub-Arctic. Those that are resident in northern regions year-round—such as the snowy owl, the gyrfalcon, the thick-billed murre, the back-legged kittiwake, and the ivory gull—don't have to go that far. Most species, however, come from mid- and southern latitudes to nest on cliffs, rock outcrops, the tundra, and wetlands. In the Yukon-Kuskokwim delta of Alaska, for example, more than a million birds fly in not only from North America, South America, and Russia but also from the plains of Africa, New Zealand, Australia, China, Japan, and Korea.

The flights of some of these birds are epic. Some peregrines that summer on the west coast of Hudson Bay fly as much as 8,000 miles from South America. Those that nest on Banks and Baffin Islands may fly even farther. Another species, the tiny, 4-ounce Arctic tern, however, is the long-distance champion. It racks up 44,000 miles on a flight that takes it from Antarctica to the Arctic each spring.

There are many reasons these birds expend so much energy to nest in a place where brief, but brutal, spring blizzards are not unusual. Once they get to places such as the Yukon-Kuskokwim and Mackenzie deltas, the Queen Maud Gulf Bird Sanctuary in Canada, Coburg Island in the High Arctic, and Sørkapp Bird Sanctuary in Svalbard, they are compensated with a burst of food that is produced by twenty-four hours of sunlight, relatively stable summer weather, the absence of many parasites that can seriously weaken or kill them, and the paucity of predators that will eat them, their chicks, or their eggs. In most of these places, there are vast tracts of pristine habitat that allow them to nest as close to, or as far away from, one another as they please.

Sometime around the late 1980s, scientists and Inuit began to notice changes in the weather, the food the birds eat, the number of parasites that were infecting them, and the predators that stalked them. Soon thereafter, it became clear that the peregrine and year-round residents like the gyrfalcon, the willow and rock ptarmigan, the long-tailed jaeger or skua, Ross's gulls, and ivory gulls were showing signs of decline or extreme stress in some parts of the Arctic. Shorebirds, by far the most numerous and species-rich among all Arctic waterbirds, were faring even worse. In 2013, scientists suggested that more than 40 percent of fifty million shorebirds birds that fly to the Arctic each year were in decline (Figure 8.1). Even common eiders and thick-billed murres—birds that are superbly adapted to extreme Arctic conditions—were having trouble adapting to the changes.

No one explanation accounts for what is happening, even if changes in the Arctic are entirely to blame. Research involving the tundra peregrine may, in part, help explain what is going on, though.

The discovery of the Rankin Inlet population of these falcons in the early 1980s by biologist Cormack Gates (the Inuit had long known that the birds were there) was a wonderful surprise. In the 1970s, the worldwide use of DDT and other organochlorines had contaminated

Figure 8.1 There is no single reason that many birds that migrate to or live year-round in the Arctic are showing signs of stress, but it's clear that climate change is contributing to the problem on a variety of levels. Photo credit: Edward Struzik

the bird's food chain and thinned its eggshells to the point where they cracked before chicks could be hatched. At one point, there were no more than a handful of these birds successfully nesting on the Great Plains and boreal forests of North America.

In the north, though, not only were tundra peregrines at Rankin Inlet producing healthy chicks at the time—presumably because of a diet relatively free of DDT—they were there in sufficient numbers to make them the second highest concentration of nesting peregrines in the world, and the highest known in Arctic regions.

Court is a big husky man with a booming voice—a dead ringer, I thought when I first met him, for a well-groomed Hell's Angel. Over the years that he has studied peregrine falcons, he has endured his share of nasty cuts and bruises. Now he wears a motorcycle helmet and gloves to prevent any serious injury to his head, eyes, and hands when breeding falcons stoop and strike. Even then, he told me, it feels like you've been hit by a hardcover book thrown from across the room.

Court was among the first of several biologists who have studied the population at Rankin Inlet—others included Mark Bradley, Robert Johnstone, Tom Duncan, and Dave Abernathy—but it was Mike Setterington who, in 2002, refused to let twenty years of annual monitoring become obsolete. Since then, Alastair Franke and a team of graduate students, assistants, and Inuit field staff have rejuvenated the project, focusing their efforts on understanding and measuring the effects of changes in climate on reproductive success and survival.

The first sign of real trouble became evident in 2005 when the peregrine population experienced almost total reproductive failure, adding insult to the overall long-term decline in productivity that had become the norm. The scientists initially suspected that changes in the amount of summer rain were the cause, but subsequently found that although the amount of rain had not changed, the frequency of rainstorms each summer had increased over time. Unlike many nesting birds, peregrines don't build a nest. Typically, they lay three or four eggs on a cliffside ledge in a small depression without any feathers or sticks to help protect the chicks after they hatch.

With their downy white coats insulating them against the cool summer air, these chicks do just fine. When it rains heavily over several days, however, many of them simply die of hypothermia as soon as the adults leave them unprotected.

Initially, Franke and his colleagues didn't have sufficient evidence to say with certainty whether rain was the cause. Then they analyzed meteorological records dating back to 1980 and placed artificial nesting boxes on cliffsides to provide shelter for some of the nests. With the help of remote cameras, they discovered that chicks in sheltered nests survived more often than those that were on natural nest ledges and exposed to the direct effects of heavy rain events.

Late spring and early summer rain is not the only challenge that nesting birds face in a future Arctic. Rapidly melting sea ice and rising sea levels have resulted in storm surges extending their reach farther inland into critical nesting habitats such as the Yukon-Kuskokwim delta. The absence of sea ice has also resulted in capelin overtaking cod as the main fish in northern Hudson Bay. This change has forced some Arctic seabirds like the thick-billed murre to fly farther afield in search of food. Even worse is that capelin are less nutritious than cod.

Canadian biologist Tony Gaston initially feared that murres and other nesting seabirds might be hit hard by this forced change in diet, but that has not turned out to be the case so far. What are hitting them hard, though, are polar bears, mosquitoes, extreme heat, and disease.

Gaston is to Arctic birds what Ian Stirling is to polar bears. He has been studying thick-billed murres and other seabirds in the Arctic since 1975. His book *Seabirds: A Natural History* is as good a natural history book as there is on the subject.

When Gaston began studying murres on Coats Island in the early 1980s, most of the polar bears he saw were hunting seals on the sea ice in the distance. Because that ice has begun to recede weeks earlier in spring, as it has been doing in southern Hudson Bay and the southern Beaufort Sea, many of those bears are taking refuge on Coats Island much earlier than they would have in the past. Hungrier than they would have been had they been hunting seals, the bears are now honing in on, and destroying, the eggs of the thick-billed murres.

The same thing is happening a few hundred kilometers north at the East Bay Bird Sanctuary, which is home to the largest common eider nesting colony in Nunavut. Biologist Sam Iverson has been conducting research there with project leader Grant Gilchrist of Environment Canada. In good years, nesting success among eiders can be as high as 70 percent, but when polar bears are present, as they have been in recent years when sea ice has retreated early, that success ranges from zero to 20 percent (Figure 8.2).

In addition, mosquitoes are hatching earlier than they have in the past, adding to the stresses on nesting birds. There have been so many mosquitoes in recent years that Gaston has seen some nesting murres die on their nests, with the blood literally sucked out of them.

In Gaston's words, the recent developments are "mind-boggling." He believes that a complete collapse of this population and others like it at the southern extremes of the Arctic is no longer a possibility but a certainty. "Maybe not in my lifetime," he says. "Without that ice, and with polar bears and mosquitoes hitting them hard, the only future in the Arctic for them is to move north."

Bad luck for these seabirds, it seems, has no bounds. In the summer of 2005, avian cholera, an insidious disease that can kill off large numbers of waterfowl in just a matter of hours, showed up at East

Figure 8.2 King eiders in North America have declined by 70 percent or more since the 1960s. Photo credit: Edward Struzik

Bay, where approximately five thousand eiders nest each year. It was the first time that the disease had struck in the eastern Arctic, and it wasn't a pretty sight.

Throughout June and most of July that summer, the daily routine of catching and tagging the birds was interrupted by the sight of dozens of birds suddenly heaving into convulsions and then collapsing. In a matter of hours, more than two hundred birds had dropped dead.

After lab rests confirmed the presence of avian cholera, Gilchrist realized that the disease was likely to strike again. Neither he nor any of the other scientists was prepared for the gruesome scene that unfolded the following year. In a matter of hours, the number of dead birds escalated from a few dozen to several hundred. The disease moved through the colony with such rapid stealth that many ducks died on their nests with their eyes wide open. As rigor mortis began to set in, hundreds of herring gulls descended, picking away at the dead. By the time it was over in two days, more than 3,500 eiders—three out of four nesting females—had succumbed to the disease.

Avian cholera was first detected in North America in the winter of 1943–1944 when the disease struck waterfowl overwintering on the Texas Panhandle. Since then, the bacterium has been steadily moving northward, reaching the Gulf of St. Lawrence in 1964 and as far north as Banks Island in the western Arctic, where it killed thirty thousand snow geese in 1995. The closest that avian cholera has come to the eastern Arctic was from 2004 to 2006 when it killed eiders in the Hudson Strait region of northern Quebec.

The possibility of the disease spreading to other regions of the Arctic, and to other types of waterfowl, is becoming a major concern to scientists, to wildlife managers, and to the Inuit who rely on birds for meat, eggs, and down feathers. If avian cholera were to recur with any degree of regularity, it could reduce numbers significantly and possibly wipe out some key colonies altogether.

The incidence of avian cholera at East Bay has dropped dramatically since 2008, but Canadian scientist Mark Forbes, who supervised the work that Sam Iverson did on nesting murres, is convinced that it is only a matter of time before it returns there and to other parts of the Arctic. As unlikely as that might seem now, he notes, three or four outbreaks of cholera that kill 30 percent or more of a colony could drive that colony to extinction if the outbreaks occurred within a decade. It doesn't help, he says, when polar bears and mosquitoes are hitting the nesting birds at the same time.

Until a decade ago, the Arctic had been largely immune to deadly disease outbreaks like the ones that are occurring with increasing regularity in the southern wildlife populations. The long, brutally cold winters have made it almost impossible for most disease-carrying birds and animals from the south to migrate north and transmit pathogens such as avian cholera, West Nile, phocine distemper, and chronic wasting disease.

With the Arctic warming faster than any other place on the planet, though, those climatic barriers are now breaking down on the tundra just as they have in the Arctic Ocean with the rapid retreat of sea ice. In some cases, the signs of changes are seemingly innocuous and are not necessarily negative. While I was participating in a raptor survey on Banks Island in 2000, we confirmed the presence of a pair of short-eared owls nesting along the shores of the Thomsen River. It was the first sighting of the species on the Arctic Islands and a good indication that this species at risk was expanding its range.

The proliferation of snow geese on Banks Island and other parts of the Arctic, however, is another matter altogether. The breeding population of the lesser snow goose is estimated to be five million birds, an increase of more than 500 percent since the mid-1970s.

The possibility that snow geese may serve as disease reservoirs in the Arctic is frightening. There are now so many geese in places such as La Perouse Bay on the west coast of Hudson Bay, at Karrak Lake in the Queen Maud Gulf Sanctuary in the central Arctic, on Banks Island in the High Arctic, and in the staging area in the National Wildlife Refuge of Alaska that there are, theoretically at least, not enough breeding grounds or staging areas to sustain them.

Somehow, though, the birds find a way of exploiting new habitat, as they must do because of the way they feed themselves. Snow geese eat almost anything that grows—grasses, sedges, willows, shrubs, and even horsetails—and they do so for up to twenty-four hours a day when they are not on their nests. They also leave almost nothing—not the seeds, stems, roots, or tubers—behind, and almost nothing nutritious grows back.

This high-fiber diet also makes them pooping machines. On the tundra, a female will excrete droppings six to fifteen times every hour.

None of this goose activity is particularly good for the salt- and freshwater lowlands that ribbon the thousands of miles of Arctic and sub-Arctic coastlines. What was once verdant habitat that sustained countless numbers of shorebirds along the west coast of Hudson Bay, for example, is now a baked brown, sometimes red or green carpet of powdery peat, damp moss, or marsh ragwort. The only things that can live in these alkaline landscapes are a few opportunistic insects and a handful of Death Valley–like plants. Even if snow geese populations crashed, it would take decades for this landscape to recover.

Threats to birds nesting in the Arctic are not solely a summertime phenomenon. With springtime advancing by two or three weeks, snowshoe hares, which are a key source of food for raptors like the gyrfalcon and snowy owl, may not be losing their white coats early enough, making them more vulnerable to predation in spring when they need to be mating and raising their young. Similarly, warmer and shorter winters are resulting in snowfall and icing events that may not be conducive to lemming, vole, and other rodent reproduction.

Biologist David Mossop has been studying birds in the Yukon for more than forty years. He is convinced that the rush of protein that flushes through the system in the form of lemmings, snowshoe hares, arctic ground squirrels, and other small mammals is what drives resident bird populations in the Arctic. "All Arctic creatures have to have sophisticated strategies in order to survive in this part of the world," he says. "Exploiting those peaks, I think, is part of the strategy."

The significance of keystone species in terrestrial and marine ecosystems in the Arctic is only beginning to be understood, partly because biologists tend to focus more on charismatic animals such as caribou, grizzly bears, wolves, polar bears, and killer whales than on lemmings, mice, and arctic cod.

As zoologist Charles Krebs has pointed out a number of times in recent years, however, consider that at Point Barrow in Alaska, lemmings consume three to six times more vegetation than the caribou do. In the boreal forest of the southwestern Yukon, snowshoe hares represent 48 percent of the biomass in contrast to the 13.6 percent and 2.6 percent that moose and bears, respectively, account for in the same region.

If microtine rodents disappeared from the tundra and the boreal forest, Krebs points out, many species of predators would go with them, and the structure of the plant community would be altered substantially. Of course, that isn't going to happen, but a phenomenon such as climate change could alter the timing and magnitude of the peaks that usually occur every few years in a way to which predators might have trouble adapting.

Krebs, for one, is skeptical, but some scientists suspect that change in snow conditions that once favored lemming reproduction may now be working against those animals in some places.

The implications of such changes in conditions were brought into sharp focus when Danish scientists described how a collapse in collared lemming cycles at two sites in Greenland between 1998 and 2010 resulted in a 98 percent decline in the snowy owl population. It was brought to the fore once again in a more dazzling way in the winter of 2013 when hundreds of these milk-white birds with luminous yellow eyes and wingspans of up to 5 feet descended on beaches, farmers' fields, city parks, and airport runways in southern Canada and the United States. By the first week of December, an unprecedented number of snowy owls had been spotted from North Dakota to Maine and from Newfoundland to South Carolina. There were so many birds in places where they had never been seen before that animal control specialists working for New York's Port Authority started shooting them, fearing that they might collide with planes taking off and landing at airports such as La Guardia.

Despite media interest that included a front-page article in the *New York Times* and scores of stories in other newspapers, no one could say with certainty what it was that had caused this irruption, the second in three years. The best guess is that it resulted from a bumper crop of lemmings in Nunavik in northern Quebec that resulted in a plethora of chicks. The snow that fell on the ground in the following months may not have had the structure required for lemmings to feed and reproduce. With so little food to go around, the youngest and most inexperienced owls simply flew south until they found a treeless landscape—an airport runway, for example—that was similar to the tundra they had left behind.

Biologist Mark Mallory has been watching these troublesome developments in southern edges of the Arctic unfold with some concern for the fulmars, murres, black guillemots, and other year-round Arctic birds that he studies in the High Arctic.

The summer of 2013 was an especially bad one for the birds that Mallory was studying. Snow, ice, and cold conditions lingered for so long that the terns, gulls, and jaegers at Nasaruvaalik Island didn't even lay eggs. It also appears that many fulmars and murres skipped breeding in the Prince Leopold Island Migratory Bird Sanctuary because their ledges were covered in snow and ice too late into the year.

For Mallory, that was not the concern.

"These particular species are all adapted to deal with this," he told me. "It wreaks havoc on scientists like me trying to recover tracking equipment or get survival measurements from banded birds, but they get by so long as it doesn't happen too often. What worries me is what's happening in the southern parts of the Arctic. If we see these heavy rain events and ecosystem changes migrating north into the High Arctic, I don't know how these birds are going to adapt."

The problem in coming up with management solutions for declining bird populations in the Arctic is that there is a dearth of information about how Arctic birds and their prey are faring throughout the circumpolar world. Very little is known, for example, about snowy owls, Ross's gulls, ivory gulls, and other Arctic birds because they are wide-ranging and difficult to track and study. In addition, some of these birds—Ross's gulls, for example—sometimes move their colonies, so not finding them in a certain place doesn't necessarily mean that anything is wrong.

What's more is that climate change may not be the only reason some birds like the ivory gull are in trouble. Mallory and his colleague Grant Gilchrist, for example, once thought that receding sea ice, which makes it increasingly difficult for these birds to forage on fish and marine invertebrates, was the main reason for the 80 percent decline that they've documented in Canada's population since the 1980s. Mallory is still convinced that it is a big problem. Receding sea ice, he says, means that there's less time for the gulls to follow bears and scavenge kills, just like polar bears are getting less time to hunt seals.

Mallory and Gilchrist, however, now have evidence to suggest that high levels of mercury, which the birds may be getting from foraging on seal carcasses left behind by polar bears, may be a factor just as it is beginning to be with birds that nest downstream of the oil sands in Alberta. "Mercury is something we think is a smoking gun," he says, "but because there are so few of the birds in Canada, it's tough to justify sampling to run experiments."

The future of birds in the Arctic doesn't necessarily have to be a gloomy one. The foresight that led to the banning of DDT in the 1970s is beginning to manifest itself in North American rules and regulations that are controlling the spread of mercury in the environment. That's good news, perhaps, for Ross's gulls and ivory gulls that forage on fish and polar bear kills. Wildlife managers in southern Canada and the United States have also liberalized hunting regulations that are at least controlling, if not reducing, the expansion of snow goose populations.

In addition, some parts of the Arctic appear to be more resilient to the changes that are occurring. Laval University scientist Gilles Gauthier, for example, has spent the last twenty-five years leading a team of scientists in a study of lemmings, snow geese, snowy owls, foxes, plants, and pretty much every other living thing on Bylot Island in the eastern Arctic, which is much colder than the western region because of the presence of sea ice and massive glaciers, and the effect on lemmings and snowy owls hasn't been dramatic. Lemming densities, for example, were very low on Bylot Island from 2002 to 2009, but they bounced back in 2011. The clutch sizes of snowy owls were also lower—by about 10 percent over eighteen years—but that decrease does not appear to be related to lemming densities.

Gauthier believes that to get a better handle on what is happening in the Arctic, he and other scientists working in the circumpolar Arctic need to set up international networks, like scientists have done with caribou, that can better track changes of all kind. Doing so has been difficult, however, because there is little funding available to support such initiatives.

Lack of funding for monitoring and research, however, should not be confused with a general unwillingness to spend money in the Arctic. It's simply a matter of priorities. Most everyone in the scientific community agrees that the cost of tracking changes in the Arctic is a pittance compared with the $300 million gravel road that the Canadian government is building to connect the Arctic town of Tuktoyaktuk to the Dempster Highway that now ends in Inuvik in the Northwest Territories or compared with the $5 billion that Royal Dutch Shell has spent drilling for oil off the coast of Alaska. They believe that a small investment now will pay huge dividends in the future.

"The warming that is coming will greatly exceed anything we have seen so far," said Gauthier when I last talked to him in the winter of 2014. "In order to understand how plants and animals can adapt to constraints brought on by rapid change, something needs to be done to better understand these linkages between different species."

Chapter 9

Drill, Baby, Drill

I N THE EPIC SEARCH for a Northwest Passage, the narratives
of explorers often described the Arctic landscape as picturesque
or sublime, depending on the place, the circumstances, and the
seasons. Ships that carried those intrepid explorers through this new
world had ominous names such as the *Terror* and *Erebus*, that dark
place between Earth and Hell. As vast, uninhabitable, and repelling
as these places sometimes were, the narratives left us with a legacy
of bewildering images that did not conform easily to our southern
perceptions.

In this schemata of Arctic landscapes, Ellef Ringnes Island may
well be closer to Hell than to Earth. Situated at the north end of the
Canadian archipelago, it is mostly flat and featureless save for a handful of salt domes that protrude from mudflats on the tundra like alien
forces rising up in a bad movie. In some places, it looks as if the devil
himself has bulldozed mine tailings through its river valleys. Piles of
churned-up rocks line the valley floors of muddy rivers. Nowhere is
there a speck of color or a hint of life, just nature in despair.

In assessing the livability of places in Canada, a government report gives the climate here a ninety-nine out of one hundred, with
one hundred being the worst it can get. By way of comparison, North

America's most northerly military base on Ellesmere Island comes in a distant second with an eighty-four. Edmonton, Canada's most northerly metropolitan center, scores a thirty-four.

Even American explorer Viljhamur Stefansson, a man who insisted that anyone could live happily in any corner of the Arctic, admitted that it was "the most barren place" he had ever seen when he sledged to the island in the summer of 1916. Stuart MacDonald, a scientist who worked at the weather station the Canadian and U.S. governments operated there from 1948 to 1978, dismissed it as "a region of utter desolation."

The only signs of life that scientists John Smol and Marianne Douglas saw when they spent a month on the island in the 1990s were some lichen-covered caribou antlers, two starving wolves desperately hunting seals, and a few lemmings nesting under the wreck of a U.S. cargo plane that crashed while trying to take off on the weather station's muddy runway with 5 inches of snow on the ground and ice building up on its wings.

I can't say that I was sorry the day we were to leave this gloomy place. The petroleum geologists I had accompanied on my trip to Ellef Ringnes were searching for signs of oil and gas that might lie beneath the tundra. What we mostly got in the short time we were there were thick fog, driving sleet, and the occasional snow squall that kept us inside our tents for a good deal of the time.

Thankfully, the skies were uncharacteristically clear the day we began knocking down our tents, packing up our gear, and draining the last drops of muddy drinking water we had brought with us. The only sign of the misery that had confined us to chilly quarters for most of our stay was a thick bank of fog on the distant horizon.

There was, however, a last-minute change of plan that was to affect me in a way that I could not have imagined that morning. Geologist Benoit Beauchamp wanted to make sure that he wouldn't miss his flights home, so he suggested that I take his place in the helicopter while he flew back with the rest of the research team in the much faster Twin Otter airplane.

"That way, you can get a get a bird's-eye view of the landscape, and I won't miss my vacation," he said.

As much as I was looking forward to a hot meal and shower, fresh clothes, some clean drinking water, and a soft bed to sleep on, there was no way that I was going to turn down an opportunity to fly for five or six hours in the whirlybird. The chances of seeing polar bears, beluga whales, musk oxen, and arctic wolves are more favorable going 110 miles per hour at 1,000 feet than they are flying above or through the clouds at a higher speed in a twin-engine airplane.

The wind was beginning to blow when we finally said our good-byes, but the bank of fog that was hovering in the distance seemed to be sitting still. So Bill Turner, the pilot, turned his back on the security of the shoreline and directed the machine over the mass of broken ice toward the invisible corner of Devon Island, where a cache of 45-gallon fuel drums lay waiting for us to fill up at the halfway point.

As reliable as GPS instruments in helicopters are, this first leg of the last part of our long journey south was not meant to be. After a half hour of flying in near-perfect weather, the wall of fog that had looked so innocuous before we had lifted off now made a ghostly move, sweeping in as spooky wisps of sea smoke before thickening into a more sinister soup of gray.

Turner didn't say a word, but I knew that we were in trouble when he slowed the helicopter to a crawl. Inside our fogged-up Plexiglas bubble, the world outside was daubed by the same gray brushstroke. These moments are critical times for a pilot, when it is often difficult to tell up from down. Survival in these cases depends on experience and training as well as on the accuracy of the helicopter's instruments. Even the most experienced pilots, however, become disoriented flying near blind in these conditions. On rare occasions, they panic, distrust what their instruments are telling them, and rely on their instincts instead.

Turner, a Newfoundlander who grew up in a world in which fog, wind, and icy rain are a familiar part of the scenery, wasn't about to make that potentially fatal mistake. Instead, he radioed the pilot of the Twin Otter, which was now somewhere in the air above the clouds heading in the same direction, to get his bird's-eye view of what lay ahead.

The news from the Twin Otter was not good. Learning that there was a lot more fog ahead, Turner decided to head back to the island that had made our short stay such a miserable one.

As wise a decision as it was, our troubles were not yet over. The fog that had stopped us from getting to Devon Island that day was just as thick going back to Ellef. A powerful tailwind was also pushing the helicopter along faster than Turner was comfortable with flying so low. The last thing that he wanted to do was to run into one of the many icebergs that we saw along the way and not have time to maneuver around it.

With just a can of sardines, a few candy bars, and no water to drink, I wasn't looking forward to another night or more on the island. Once I saw goose feathers swirling up beneath us, though, I caught myself sighing in relief. Neither one of us could see the ground just then, but the feathers were a sure sign that we had made it back to land.

My trip to Ellef Ringnes had begun ten days earlier when I had hitched a three-hour ride on a Twin Otter from the Canadian Polar Continental Shelf Research Base at Resolute on Cornwallis Island to Eureka, which is picturesquely located in the shadow of the Sawtooth Mountains at the north end of Ellesmere Island. Turner was already at the Environment Canada weather station there getting ready to fly north to move Beauchamp and Steve Grasby, a geologist with the Geological Survey of Canada, from their camp on the north end of Ellesmere to Ellef Ringnes.

Beauchamp, Grasby, and their two students made up one of several government-sponsored geological teams that had come north that summer to continue mapping the energy and mineral potential of the Arctic.

As bleak and repelling a place as Ellef Ringnes is, there is the potential for an enormous amount of oil and gas to be found here and in the more picturesque parts of the circumpolar world. The most conservative and comprehensive estimates come from the U.S. Geological Survey. Scientists there have calculated that there are 90 billion barrels of undiscovered, technically recoverable oil, 1,670 trillion cubic feet of technically recoverable natural gas, and 44 billion barrels of technically recoverable natural gas liquids. That would account for about 22 percent of the undiscovered, technically recoverable resources in the world.

Put another way, the Arctic holds about 13 percent of the undiscovered oil, 30 percent of the undiscovered natural gas, and 20 percent of the undiscovered natural gas liquids in the world. That does not include the energy reserves stored in gas hydrates in the Arctic, which exceed those of any major gas field in the world (Figure 9.1).

Ellef Ringnes didn't quite live up to the image that I was expecting when we first landed there. Instead of fog, sleet, clouds, and the hellish landscape I was anticipating, we landed on a 50-meter-high plateau at Dumbbells Dome with sunshine radiating down on yellow arctic poppies and a couple of caribou.

All that changed a few hours later when a wall of fog and cold rain moved in, reducing visibility to just a few hundred meters. Huddling in from the cold that first night on the island, it became clear to me that the big government-funded budget that these frontier geologists were drawing from wasn't temptation enough to get them to abandon their reputation as a band of rugged, bean-eating rock doctors who think nothing of going a month without a shower.

Beauchamp was happily slicing green mold off a couple of blocks of cheese that first night while Grasby poured muddy water into a kettle to make tea. As the guest of honor, I was invited to be the first to dip into a couple of $4 cans of smoked oysters that were served with soggy crackers and a thimble of Scotch that was carefully rationed from a small and dwindling supply.

As low on fuel as we were by then, there was no talk of warming the tent up that night with the stove even though the temperature was only few degrees above the freezing mark. "Water is going to be the big issue next year when we bring in a bigger camp of people," Grasby observed. "There's a lot of shale on this island. Shale tends to generate muddy water, which is very hard to filter. What little clean water there is is very high in sulfates. At the levels we find here on the island, they can act as a diuretic. That may explain why oil field workers who were here in the 1970s were always complaining about having the runs. Apparently, more than one cook lost his job when the crew manager suspected it was the food that was the cause."

On first impression, Grasby struck me as a bit like Mr. Spock, a foil to Beauchamp's gregarious Captain Kirk. Tall, slim, and bearded, Grasby spoke in matter-of-fact terms, much as a geologist or a mathematician might in front of a classroom of students. Nothing his former mentor and teacher did or said was outrageous enough to get his adrenalin going.

Figure 9.1 Receding sea ice in the Arctic is revealing a treasure trove of energy resources that were once inaccessible. Scientists, conservationists, and some Inuit leaders believe that the pace of development is proceeding too quickly and without rules, regulations, and standards to prevent spills and accidents. Photo credit: Edward Struzik

It wasn't long, however, before I saw another side to his personality. Mostly, it was through the stories he told about his wife, children, and great aunt.

Grasby clearly admired his wife for being so unlike him. She didn't think twice about buying a house or a dog without telling him or setting off on two-week family vacations without any firm plans in place.

Grasby also had a soft spot for a great aunt who raised Shetland ponies in Britain. She allowed the animals to eat and sleep in the kitchen, but she made him and his father sleep outside in a trailer when they visited. This great aunt was locally famous for teaching John Lennon to handle horses and for producing a pony for the Italian dictator Benito Mussolini.

As gregarious as Beauchamp was in comparison, it was evident that he is very serious about the future of the Arctic and how his research will be used to shape it.

"The North American Arctic is clearly in the crosshairs of the energy industry," he told me that night. "It's only a matter of time before the start of a new era of energy exploration is under way. Conventional supplies of energy are drying up just as the economies of India and China are catching fire."

What the future of the Arctic will look like in this era of rapid change will be even more uncertain as this frontier energy is exploited by energy interests. Not only does the industry have a long history of oil spills and gas blowouts in the region, it has no effective way of cleaning up oil that comes into contact with ice. Should a spill occur in the future, as it inevitably will, recovery in summer will be extremely slow, let alone impossible should the spill or blowout linger into the dark, cold months of winter.

Even as scientists struggle to understand how this polar ecosystem will respond to climate change, Arctic governments are using it to give industry the green light to frack on land and to drill offshore in the deepest and most remote parts of the Arctic. Confident that everything will be okay when the science suggests otherwise, decision makers are giving serious consideration to easing precautionary measures that will stop the flow of oil and gas should a blowout or accident occur. No one, it seems, is seriously thinking about an *Exxon Valdez* spill or a Deepwater Horizon drilling rig blowout even though the past tells us that environmental disasters such as those will be part of the future.

Initially, I didn't know what to expect when I first met up with these geologists who were there on Ellef Ringnes to help industry find what they are looking for. Beauchamp, I knew, hasn't exactly been a fan of the media ever since news gatherers from around the world went on a feeding frenzy over his discovery of alien-like bacteria percolating from a mountain glacier on Ellesmere Island several years ago. The find was a remarkable one because it might someday serve as an analog for how life got its start here on Earth and on other places in the galaxy. Some of the media reports, however, were so over the top that it sounded like Beauchamp had found proof that there are tiny extraterrestrials living deep down in the Arctic's frozen underworld.

Judging from our previous discussions on the telephone, Grasby also seemed to have doubts about me coming along. Perhaps I was wrong, but I got the distinct impression that he had concerns about a journalist participating in a government-funded science project that could lead to intense development of an Arctic that most environmentalists and some Inuit leaders would like to see remain pristine (Figure 9.2).

Since its inception in 2008, Geo-mapping for Energy and Minerals, the federally funded program in Canada that brings Beauchamp, Grasby, and dozens of other petroleum geologists to the Arctic each year, has spent more than $100 million of taxpayers' money to help the energy and mining industries find new sources of fossil fuels and minerals in the region. With another $100 million promised as of 2013, the subsidy will continue until 2020.

Canada is not alone in going out of its way to court frontier energy and mineral development. It is, however, leading the pack of nations with interests in the Arctic. Not only is Canada building a road to resources from Inuvik to Tuktoyaktuk at taxpayers' expense, it offered to pay the $50,000-a-day cost of escorting a Danish cargo ship (filled with coal, of all things) through the Northwest Passage in 2013. The ship's owners were more than happy to oblige because it allowed their vessel to carry 25 percent more coal than would have been possible through the shallower Panama Canal, where freighters must sail higher in the water. The captain of the *Nordic Orion* was also able to shave about four days of travel time by traveling this shorter route. That added another $1 million to the savings.

In many ways, concerns about the energy industry's effect on the Arctic environment are as justifiable today as they were in 1989 when the hard-drinking skipper of the *Exxon Valdez* steered the oil tanker off course before striking Bligh Reef in Prince William Sound in Alaska and approximately 11 million gallons of crude oil was spilled. The multibillion-dollar cleanup that followed was one of the worst manmade disasters in North American history.

More than $2 billion was spent over four years to clean things up. The environmental effect, however, lingered much longer than anyone had anticipated. In 2001, a team from the National Oceanic and Atmospheric Administration (NOAA), which surveyed ninety-six sites along 8,000 miles of coastline, found approximately 20 acres of

Figure 9.2 Geologist Steve Grasby examines rocks on Ellef Ringnes Island where oil and gas companies were operating in the 1970s. Photo credit: Edward Struzik

shoreline in Prince William Sound still contaminated with oil. The team also found signs of oil at 58 percent of the sites assessed.

In a civil settlement with the U.S. government, Exxon agreed to pay $900 million in payments, $100 million in restitution, and a $25 million fine. In 2013, however, the U.S. Justice Department and State of Alaska were still waiting to collect a final $92 million claim so that they could deal with unanticipated damages that were done to fish, wildlife, and habitat in the region.

The *Exxon Valdez* may have been the most memorable environmental disaster in the Arctic and sub-Arctic world, but contrary to public perception and industry assurances, spills, blowouts, and accidents have plagued the search for oil and gas episodically since the late 1960s when oil was found on the north slope of Alaska at Prudhoe Bay.

A report commissioned by Alaska's governor following the spill in Alaska summed it up succinctly: "The *Exxon Valdez* was not an isolated, freak occurrence, but simply one result of policies, habits and practices that for nearly two decades have infused the nation's maritime oil transportation system with increasing levels of risk. The *Exxon Valdez* was an accident waiting to happen."

It was a Wild West show back then not only in Alaska but also in Arctic Canada. There were few rules to follow, almost no penalties for breaking those that were on the books, and no respect for more than one hundred scientists who concluded in a landmark, multivolume study in 1977 that no one has the "capacity to contain or clean up oil that may be spilled in the North."

I could see the signs of this laissez-faire approach almost everywhere I flew in the Arctic that summer with Beauchamp and Grasby. Piles of rusty fuel drums, broken-down machinery, and debris were scattered everywhere. Many of the truck and tractor tire tracks I saw at abandoned exploration camps on Devon, Ellesmere, Ellef Ringnes, and other islands looked as if they had been made the year before.

All this action began in 1968 when the Canadian government, envious of the enormous amount of oil that had been found at Prudhoe Bay in Alaska, embarked on a decades-long program to encourage exploration of its Arctic. Panarctic Oil Ltd., which consolidated the interests of more than seventy companies and individuals, was formed to do what the government, the major shareholder in this case, wanted done.

The National Energy Program that followed during the international energy crisis of the 1970s was designed to make Canada energy self-sufficient. To that end, the Canadian government spent $1.5 billion to create Petro Canada, a Crown corporation, which was also given the government's 45 percent stake in Panarctic Oil Ltd. and its 12 percent stake in Syncrude, now an oil sands giant.

Under the Petroleum Incentive Program, which was a cornerstone of the National Energy Program, companies were reimbursed up to 80 percent of the cost of wells drilled in frontier areas. Additional incentives resulted in some companies getting all their exploration money back.

Money flowed like water in those days. Hundreds of wells were drilled in areas where there was a relatively low probability of success. Oil field crews lived the high life with live lobsters being flown in seasonally once a week to the base camp at Tuktoyaktuk. At one point, the gravel airstrip at Rea Point on the uninhabited island of Melville was busier than the landing strips at Edmonton, the capital city of Alberta.

Panarctic alone drilled 175 wells, fourteen of them on Ellef Ringnes. It was estimated that nineteen of the most promising discoveries held 17.5 trillion cubic feet of natural gas and some oil. None of this gas ever made it to market, largely because the cost and logistics associated with piping it down south made it unrealistic, and only a small amount of oil made it south, in a single-hulled tanker.

As much money as there was to do pretty much whatever industry wanted, companies such as Panarctic were often unprepared to deal with the challenges they faced when drilling for oil and gas in this polar world. Part of the problem was technology. Drilling techniques that worked in Texas and in Alberta didn't necessarily work in the Arctic. Logistics were also an issue. No one, for example, seriously considered what would happen if there was a serious oil spill or a gas well blowout in the autumn or winter months when the Arctic is dark for twenty-four hours a day and frozen solid by −40 degree Fahrenheit temperatures.

Panarctic quickly found that out when two of its wells erupted in 1969 and 1970. The first explosion occurred at Drake Point on Melville Island while crews were replacing a worn-out drill pipe. The plume of mud, water, and gas that unexpectedly surged to the surface sent everyone running to safety. As much as 40,000 barrels of saltwater and 40 million cubic feet of gas were being pumped to the surface daily. All told, it took crews sixteen months to cut off the flow.

The blowout that followed on King Christian Island was even more spectacular. When the well there blew out of control in October 1970, it released gas at ten times the flow at Drake Point. The fireball was so intense that it burned up the equivalent of 2.5 million gallons of gasoline per day. When frozen ground around the camp cracked and collapsed in some places, more than two hundred oil field workers were forced to take refuge on the sea ice. A jet plane carrying a load of men and supplies barely got off the runway in an attempt to escape the spreading inferno.

Attempts to cap the well were further complicated by the absence of roads and a nearby port or town to ferry people and equipment in and out. The cleanup and the capping crew were as vulnerable to the unpredictable weather conditions back then as Bill Turner and I were on our return to Ellef Ringnes that summer.

All told, the well on King Christian spewed gas and fire for more than three months before it was finally brought under control. Few people today are aware of it, but it remains the biggest natural gas well blowout in Canadian history.

Panarctic and other companies carried on as they always had, however, largely because there was almost no serious oversight in place nor any meaningful media coverage of what had happened. It likely didn't help that the Canadian government held a stake in the company. Blowouts continued, oil spilled on the ground and wasn't cleaned up, and waste steel, waste oil, and broken-down trucks were dumped into the ocean rather than piled up and taken back south on ships or barges.

Who knows how long Panarctic might have gotten away with this flagrant abuse of the environment had one of its own employees not blown the whistle on its practice of dumping debris, machinery, and waste into the ocean? Even then, it may have escaped with a slap on the wrist at the ensuing trial in 1983 as it and other companies had in the past had the judge presiding over the case not pushed the limits of his authority.

I had first met Judge Michel Bourassa in Yellowknife when he was one of maybe two or three frontier judges who were clearly concerned with the manner in which energy and mining companies were operating in the Arctic in the 1970s and 1980s. The $150,000 fine that he levied against Panarctic was, at the time, the biggest pollution fine in Canadian history.

Normally, judges leave it to politicians, academics, and conservation groups to comment on environmental policy. Bourassa, however, was so troubled by what was going on that he did some sleuthing himself, privately talking to government inspectors, to me, and to senior bureaucrats who were charged with keeping a watch on the industry.

"In many instances, industry plays what appears to be a deliberate strategy of manipulation—making marginal offers and increasing them incrementally," Bourassa wrote in a paper that was probably read by only a handful of legal experts. "The process of dealing with infractions becomes a negotiable matter, described to me by a senior field agent in the Environmental Protection Service as akin to buying a used car, involving bluff, posturing and pressure. In this atmosphere of constant negotiation, bickering, offer and counter-offer, we tend to lose sight of the bottom line: there has apparently been an offence—an important law has been broken."

It would be "naive," Bourassa added, "to pretend that industries are without political influence and capable of bringing enormous pressure to bear on politicians, and through them on regulatory bodies. Political or bureaucratic pressure to compromise with an offender, or not to prosecute, will remain a fact of life. That regulatory agencies will, in one way or another, react to this pressure is equally self-evident."

Some things have improved since Bourassa's groundbreaking fine and in the aftermath of the *Exxon Valdez*. For instance, in Prince William Sound, there are now trained, on-call fishing vessels on hand that can provide an immediate response to an oil spill. There are also plans in place to deal with spilled oil once it's recovered. One approach uses helium-filled balloons carrying both infrared and conventional cameras tethered to cleanup and response vessels to supplement traditional overflights during a response.

The oil spill cleanup capabilities in Prince William Sound, however, are unique. In the larger scheme of things north of the 60th parallel, the energy industry is no better prepared to prevent or to deal effectively with an oil spill than they were when the *Exxon Valdez* hit that reef in 1989. In addition, as recent spills, blowouts, and pipeline ruptures in the south have shown, regulatory regimes and industry's ability to prevent and clean up spills continue to be insufficient.

That fact came into sharp focus on April 20, 2010, when an explosion caused by a blowout on the Deepwater Horizon drilling rig in the Gulf of Mexico owned by British Petroleum (BP) resulted in the largest offshore oil spill in U.S. history. Eleven people were killed, and untold damage was done to the environment. Legal wrangling, which is expected to last for at least another decade, has become so unwieldy that one legal expert quipped that "it reads like a novel."

The Deepwater Horizon and *Exxon Valdez* disasters, of course, were different in the ways that they unfolded, but many of those who were involved in the investigation of the *Exxon Valdez* believe that history repeated itself in the Gulf of Mexico because lessons that were learned after 1989 have gone unheeded. "It's disappointing," Walter Parker, the man who chaired the Alaska Oil Spill Commission, told the *Washington Post*. "It's as though we had never written the report."

BP, of course, described it as a freak accident in which a "complex and interlinked series of mechanical failures, human judgments, engineering design, operational implementation and team interfaces came together to allow the initiation and escalation of the accident." Another way of looking at it is that the company pushed the envelope too far by failing, or perhaps refusing, to appreciate that safety margins must reflect the heightened risks associated with drilling as deeply as they did in the Gulf of Mexico. The Deepwater Horizon crew, in this case, wrongly interpreted two pressure tests that were done to see if hydrocarbons were flowing in the well that had been cemented. As smart as they were, they could not see what was happening so far below them.

The same might be said about energy companies drilling in the Arctic where sea ice, twenty-four hours of winter darkness, intense cold, and severe weather complicate even the simplest of drilling plans. For these and other reasons, after Deepwater Horizon both Canadian and U.S. agencies began to examine whether regulatory standards were sufficient to prevent an oil spill from happening in the Arctic.

The verdict in each case was the same. Organizations such as the Ocean Energy Safety Advisory Committee, NOAA, and the National Energy Board (NEB)—Canada's main regulatory agency—concluded that regulatory standards needed to be overhauled to deal with the unique Arctic environment in which energy companies were drilling for oil.

Surprisingly, the NEB, often seen as too friendly to the energy industry that provides most of its funding—went one step farther when it noted that there was a "common thread" in the root causes of the many accidents that have occurred in the Canadian Arctic in the past. In its own words, it stated that there was "a neglect of, or even an absence of, processes and procedures to identify, mitigate, or eliminate potential risks."

"Beneath that deficiency," the NEB report added, "lies an even deeper pattern of organizational cultures that did not put safety first.

An organization's safety culture is made up of individual employee and group beliefs, values, attitudes, and behaviors about safety." The NEB promised that any company wishing to drill in the Arctic, "must have a strong safety culture."

The other thing that the Deepwater Horizon accident did was raise concern about the boats, equipment, and infrastructure that are needed to deal with a major oil spill, a gas well blowout, or an accident in the Arctic. As difficult as it was to bring the Deepwater Horizon blowout under control in open water where ships, barges, and helicopters could be easily flown in and out, it would be much more difficult, if not impossible, to deal with a similar crisis in the Arctic. It would be especially difficult if the oil were spilling under thick ice offshore from an island as remote and difficult to get to as Ellef Ringnes or if the spill were to occur during a storm that was as intense and long-lasting as the cyclone of 2012.

Canada still does not have a deepwater port in the Arctic from which to stage a cleanup. In the relatively shallow waters of the Chukchi Sea, the closest U.S. Coast Guard base is more than 1,000 miles away. Oil prevention and mitigation capacity in the region is lacking. Fully modern charts that would facilitate safer shipping in northern Canada do not exist for many places.

The implications of these deficiencies were spelled out in the aftermath of Deepwater Horizon by a group of Arctic conservation organizations. Comparing the first twenty-four hours of the Deepwater Horizon response to the assets that Shell planned for the first twenty-four hours of a response to a spill or blowout in the Chukchi, the group observed the following:

- Within twenty-four hours of the Deepwater Horizon blowout, 32 spill-response vessels were mobilized. By way of comparison, only thirteen would have been available in the Chukchi Sea.
- Skimming capacity in the Gulf of Mexico was 171,000 barrels per day. In the Chukchi, it was 24,000 barrels per day.
- In the Gulf of Mexico, the offshore storage capacity was 122,000 barrels, with another 175,000 barrels on standby. In the Chukchi, storage capacity was a mere 28,000 barrels.

- In the Chukchi Sea, fewer than 6,000 feet of containment boom were available. In the Gulf of Mexico, there were 417,320 feet of boom available.

Conservation organizations such as the U.S. Center for Biological Diversity and Greenpeace are categorically opposed to offshore drilling in the Arctic. Groups like the World Wildlife Fund and the Pew Charitable Trusts advocate for a balance between responsible energy development and environmental protection. For this balance to be achieved, Marilyn Heiman, a former U.S. Interior Department official who now serves as director of Pew's U.S. Arctic Project, strongly advocates for the U.S. establishment of world-class Arctic standards for offshore drilling that would account for the region's remoteness, lack of infrastructure, and harsh climate. Pew's 2013 report on Arctic standards recommends that vessels, drilling rigs, and facilities be built to withstand maximum ice forces. Equipment needed to control a spill, such as relief rigs and well-control containment systems, should be designed for and located in the Arctic so that they can be readily deployed. The report also recommends that offshore exploration drilling be restricted to the ice-free season.

Several groups, including the Pew Charitable Trusts and the World Wildlife Fund, have compiled and proposed the best science to ensure—in addition to strong standards for offshore drilling hotspots that are integral to Inuit subsistence hunting, marine mammals, and migratory bird migration and high-use areas and ecosystems resilience—that certain areas should be off-limits to drilling altogether.

Even the U.S. Navy and Canadian military have raised concerns about their ability to respond to a crisis in the Arctic. Neither Canada nor the United States currently has the necessary icebreaker capabilities to adequately respond to an oil spill or a natural gas blowout in the region. The U.S. Coast Guard has two existing heavy polar icebreakers, the *Polar Star* and the *Polar Sea*, and both have exceeded their thirty-year service lives. The *Polar Star* was placed in caretaker status from 2006 to 2009 when Congress provided funding to repair it. It was returned to service in December 2012. Coast Guard officials are crossing their fingers that those repairs will be sufficient to keep the ship operational for another five years or so.

The reason is simple. In June 2010, the Coast Guard's second heavy icebreaker, the *Polar Sea*, suffered an unexpected engine casualty. It was placed in commissioned, inactive status on October 14, 2011. A third, less powerful icebreaker, *Healy*, is still in use, but it is used mainly for scientific research. It cannot do what *Polar Sea* and *Polar Star* do in thick ice.

In a report presented to Congress in July 2013, Ronald O'Rourke, a U.S. naval specialist, described the potential consequences of having only one heavy icebreaker available to do all that might need to be done in ensuring that all is well in the Arctic.

"No matter how technologically advanced or efficiently operated, a single polar icebreaker can operate in the Polar Regions for only a portion of any year," he wrote. "An icebreaker requires regular maintenance and technical support from shipyards and industrial facilities, must reprovision regularly, and has to effect periodic crew changeouts. A single icebreaker, therefore, could not meet any reasonable standard of active and influential presence and reliable, at-will access throughout the polar regions.

"A second consideration," he noted, "is the potential risk of failure in the harsh conditions of polar operations. Despite their intrinsic robustness, damage and system failure are always a risk and the U.S. fleet must have enough depth to provide backup assistance. Having only a single icebreaker would necessarily require the ship to accept a more conservative operating profile, avoiding more challenging ice conditions because reliable assistance would not be available. A second capable icebreaker, either operating elsewhere or in homeport, would provide ensured backup assistance and allow for more robust operations by the other ship."

As it has in the past, Canada could help the United States in a pinch, but its icebreakers are not in good shape either. The *Louis St. Laurent*, the flagship of a small group of aging icebreakers, has had so many makeovers that crew members jokingly refer to her as the "Joan Rivers of the Fleet." The Canadian government has plans to build a new icebreaker, but recent delays suggest that it won't be operational until at least 2020–2021 and possibly much later.

Despite all that is being said by scientists, environmentalists, native leaders, regulatory agencies, and the military, the energy industry

continues to downplay the possibility that something might go hor-
ribly wrong with drilling in the Arctic. In 2010, companies with interests in the region went to court to block the Obama administration's
plan to protect 183,000 square miles of polar bear habitat off the coast
of Alaska. Then, in 2011, David Lawrence, executive vice president
of Shell, which has invested $6 billion in exploration in the Chukchi
Sea, insisted that the challenges of drilling in the Arctic are "relatively
easy."

Those were famous last words for a man who abruptly left the
company after a series of blunders that included the near-grounding
of one of its drill rigs, a fire on the same rig, the failure of its oil spill
containment dome, and the grounding of a drilling rig on a pristine,
wildlife-rich island in Alaska in December 2012.

Shell's record of performance in the Arctic was so bad in so many
ways that U.S. Interior Secretary Ken Salazar summed it up by bluntly
saying: "Shell screwed up in 2012 and we are not going to let them
screw up after their pause is removed. Shell will not be able to move
forward into the Arctic to do any kind of exploration unless they have
this integrated management plan put in place."

Lessons of the past suggest that the most prudent thing to do is
to take a time-out, as Shell was forced to do. Time-outs would mean
waiting until Canada and the United States build new icebreakers as
well as the infrastructure that is needed to deal effectively with an
emergency in the Arctic. Canada also needs one or more deepwater
ports from which cleanups and emergency responses can be staged.
State-of-the-art navigation aids need to be put in place, and modern
navigation charts are required to facilitate all the shipping that will
come with resource development, fishing, and tourism development.
Most of all, rules for drilling should no longer be discretionary as they
seem to be in both countries. It should be clear to all what is required
to drill in the Arctic and what the effects will be if there is an accident.

In the end, rational decision makers may conclude, as Rebecca
Noblin of the U.S. Center for Biological Diversity has done, that
there should be no drilling in the Arctic. That, however, is wishful
thinking. Oil knows no boundaries, as the oil sands in Alberta have
proven. Hooked on revenues that come from oil, decision makers can't
resist once the money comes rolling in.

It's impossible to be completely prepared for all that might come in a future Arctic, but it is at the very least worth trying to figure out where those "no-go" boundaries might be and how we might better prevent accidents or deal with them when they do occur. As the Alaska tundra fire of 2007 and the great Arctic cyclone of 2012 demonstrated, there are going to be surprises for which we are not prepared.

The more immediate problem, however, is that we are not the least bit prepared for events that we know will happen. For political rather than economic reasons, the science that is needed to help us prepare for the future Arctic is lagging far behind the pace of oil, gas, and mining activity in the region.

Consider, for example, the pace of exploration that followed after the pause that came as a result of Deepwater Horizon.

In 2012, Canada awarded eight new exploration licenses to energy companies in the Mackenzie River valley, the Beaufort Sea, and the Mackenzie delta. Another two were issued to Shell Canada Limited and MGM Energy Corp in the central Mackenzie valley. The licenses cover more than 150,000 hectares land. In the Beaufort Sea, six off-shore exploration licenses covering more than 900,000 hectares were awarded to Franklin Petroleum Limited.

In 2013, the NEB gave Conoco permission to drill and horizontally frack two wells in the Mackenzie valley. It was the first time that the regulator had permitted horizontal fracking in the North, and it did so just months after a Council of Canadian Academies expert review report suggesting that more research is required to understand the effect that fracking may have on the environment was issued.

That same year, Imperial, Exxon Mobil Corporation, and BP p.l.c. filed a project description with Canadian regulators as the first step in a plan to drill in the deepest water yet on the Canadian side of the Beaufort Sea.

Had it not been for a court case that environmental and native groups had successfully launched and won in the United States, Shell would have returned to the Arctic in the summer of 2014. The decision in that case came from the U.S. Court of Appeals for the Ninth Circuit in January 2014. The judge ruled that the Department of the Interior violated the law when it sold offshore oil and gas leases in the Chukchi Sea. The decision stemmed from a lawsuit filed by a coalition of Alaska native and conservation groups made up of the Native Village of Point Hope, Inupiat Community of the Arctic Slope, Alaska Wilderness League, Center for Biological Diversity, Defenders of Wildlife, National Audubon Society, and Natural Resources Defense Council.

For every case that is won by environmental and native organizations, though, governments and industry seem to find ways of getting what they desire.

In 2010, for example, a Canadian court issued an injunction to stop seismic testing in Lancaster Sound, where plans for an Arctic national marine park have been under way for decades. The injunction forced a German research vessel that was involved in the testing to change its route midway through its voyage. Inuit in places such as Arctic Bay and Pond Inlet on Baffin Island feared that the sounds that come with the seismic activity would frighten off or injure belugas, narwhals, and bowheads in the region.

In late June 2014, however, the Canadian government approved an even more aggressive exploration plan in the region. Shocked by the development, an Inuit leader echoed the concerns of other leaders in the Arctic. "They still don't get it," said Okalik Eegeesiak, president of the Qikiqtani Inuit Association. "They still don't get the fact that Inuit have concerns and we want to be part of the process. When we're part of the process we are likely to support it more."

It also seems that the NEB is no longer so concerned about the deeper pattern of organizational cultures that did not put safety first in the Arctic. In 2013, the NEB expressed willingness to consider giving companies an exemption to a regulation that requires the drilling of a relief well, like the one that was belatedly drilled to finally bring the Deepwater Horizon blowout under control.

Few people seemed to see the irony in it being ExxonMobil and BP that were the most vocal opponents of the relief well regulation. The two companies are now partnering in drilling plans in the Beaufort Sea that rival the depths at which Deepwater Horizon drilled in the Gulf of Mexico.

Given the uncertainty that exists in an Arctic world that is rapidly changing, one would have expected that the Arctic Council would have addressed the issue of oil spills, cleanup procedures, and the mapping of biological hotspots that should be off-limits to drill-ing. Instead, the agreement that eight Arctic countries—Canada, the United States, Russia, Finland, Sweden, Norway, Iceland, and Den-mark (representing dependencies Greenland and the Faroe Islands)—signed in May 2013 was remarkably vague in detailing how this would play out in the future.

Under this agreement, each country is required to maintain a na-tional system for responding to oil pollution incidents, including a national contingency plan providing for an organizational relationship of the various bodies involved (public or private) that takes relevant laws and guidelines into account. The parties must furthermore estab-lish a minimum level of prepositioned oil spill combating equipment, a program of exercises for oil pollution response organizations and the training of relevant personnel, plans and communications capabilities for responding to an oil pollution incident, and a mechanism or ar-rangement to coordinate the response.

More than a year later, a U.S. National Research Council commit-tee came out with a 183-page report that underscored that Arctic na-tions are not even close to being prepared for an oil spill in the region. Citing *Exxon Valdez*, Deepwater Horizon, and Shell's mishaps in the Arctic, the panel of experts succinctly pointed out that we need to know more about the Arctic. We need to spill oil on purpose to deter-mine the best ways of cleaning it up. We need a better-equipped Coast Guard and a plan for wildlife. The panel also noted that the United States needs to start working with Russia, which is determined to see more ships passing through the northern sea route via Bering Strait. The panel should have recommended the addition of Canada in those discussions, given the country's recent efforts to promote shipping through the Northwest Passage.

Chapter 10

The Need for an Arctic Treaty

I N THE SPRING OF 2010, I was camped on a fragile ice floe close to where the North Magnetic Pole once was before it continued to drift toward Russian territory. During the time I was there, the wind-chill temperature never rose above −30 degrees Fahrenheit. Sleep did not come easy in a tent that was forever flapping in the wind, nor did the eating of meals I lined up for in the steamy air of a frozen Quonset hut. The one shower I had was little more than a spray of water that was made warmish by the exhaust of groaning diesel generators.

With me were forty men and women: scientists, engineers, and pilots with military and civilian backgrounds. Collectively, they had been assigned the task of cleaning toilets, washing floors, plowing snow, cutting giant holes in the ice, and redrawing the map of the future Arctic in Canada's favor by the end of 2013.

As uncertain as the future of polar bears, caribou, belugas, birds, and other animals is in a future Arctic, the lines that define the boundaries between nations that have maritime borders there are becoming increasingly clear. Under the United Nations Convention on the Law of the Sea (UNCLOS), a country can lay claim to the ocean floor beyond the internationally recognized 200-nautical-mile limit. To do so, it has to prove that the seabed is an extension of its continental shelf.

Until a couple of decades ago, Canada, the United States, Russia, Norway, and Denmark—the five coastal Arctic states with legitimate claims—showed very little interest in doing so because there didn't seem to be anything of value in the unclaimed regions of the Arctic. Now that receding sea ice is revealing a potential treasure trove of oil, gas, minerals, and a potential future fishery, however, each country is spending hundreds of millions of dollars in the hopes of adding millions of square miles to their Arctic boundaries (Figure 10.1).

Everything had gone according to plan for Canada that spring until it was time to launch a 24-foot-long torpedo-shaped submersible that had been flown up in pieces before being put together on the ice floe we were camped on.

With an acoustic modem on board that sends out data showing where it is, how fast it's going, and what the seafloor looks like, the submersible—better known as an AUV, for autonomous underwater vehicle—was supposed to make its inaugural 60-mile round trip to map the ocean floor near the edge of Canada's northern boundaries within a twenty-three-hour period.

It didn't.

Around 10:20 p.m. that evening, the same group of men and women that had lowered the AUV beneath the thick ice fifteen hours earlier were standing around, listening in vain for the distinctive electronic chirp that was expected after the submersible reversed course and came within range of the camp's underwater sensors.

Realizing that it was overdue and possibly in trouble, team leaders discussed the prospects of sending one or more of the four helicopters on-site to find the AUV beneath a sea of ice that was slowly breaking up in some places and swirling in unpredictable directions in others.

The last thing that anyone wanted to do in the frigid twilight hours of the polar night was to drill holes through 6 to 15 feet of ice every 3 to 5 miles to home in on a signal. Even if the group were successful in detecting the signal and finding where it was coming from, the prospects of pulling a disabled AUV out of the water in such a remote spot would have been daunting.

It was not what then Canadian Foreign Affairs Minister Lawrence

Figure 10.1 This Canadian base camp is located off the coast of Borden Island in the High Arctic. Canada, the United States, Russia, Norway, and Denmark are redrawing the map of the polar world, with claims to territory that currently belongs to no one. Photo credit: Edward Struzik

Cannon had in mind when he flew up to the Arctic the day before to see how Canada was investing $200 million in a five-year mapping project.

Cannon was still smarting from the very public scolding he had received from Hillary Clinton, then U.S. secretary of state, who believed that Canada was wrong in not inviting Inuit leaders and three other Arctic countries to participate in a meeting that it was hosting on the future of the Arctic. The minister was also sensitive about intelligence reports suggesting that the Russians might upstage Canada's mission here by dropping paratroopers at the North Pole in the days or weeks ahead.

Putting on a brave face when he eventually landed at that ice camp near Borden Island, Cannon downplayed Clinton's remarks and dismissed the Russian drop at the North Pole as a publicity stunt.

"We know Canadian Rangers will be up here," he said, making reference to a small group of Inuit hunters who act as the military's eyes and ears in the Arctic. "So if the Russians have any difficulties, obviously Canada will come to their rescue. We'll be available to help them. Science will decide who owns the Arctic. Not stunts like this."

One would have thought that after five years of mapping the ocean floor, there would have been no surprises when it was time for Canada to finally submit its claim in December 2013. Surprise, though, as well as dismay, is how Canadian Prime Minister Stephen Harper reacted when he reviewed Canada's submission, presumably for the first time, on the eve of it being sent to UNCLOS. Seeing that the North Geographic Pole was not included, he ordered the mappers to go back to the drawing board.

Russia's president, Vladimir Putin, was evidently not amused. His country had already made its case for the pole in a 2001 submission to UNCLOS that was sent back to Russia for further research. This last-minute intervention by the Canadian prime minister was seen as an affront. As if to underline his displeasure, Putin ordered, or re-ordered in this case, the military to deploy two hundred aircraft, forty intercontinental ballistic missiles, and two nuclear submarines to the region. He also repeated a previous vow to reopen Cold War bases in the Arctic.

"I would like you to devote special attention to deploying infra-structure and military units in the Arctic," Putin stated in televised comments at a meeting of the Defense Ministry Board in Moscow that week. "The country requires every lever for the protection of its security and national interests there."

It was hard to know what to make of his words, as I was asked to do by a major Russian television station that week.

"Will this lead to an escalation of conflict in the Arctic?" the television news host wanted to know.

As unlikely as that is in the present or the foreseeable future, I didn't know what to say. Even though the Russians have been playing by UNCLOS rules, they have a habit of chest thumping when it comes to staking claims in the Arctic. In 2007, when Russia's own mapping team deposited a Russian flag, cast in rust-free titanium, on the seafloor beneath the North Pole, the event was choreographed and filmed in a manner that was clearly intended to announce to the world, and to the Russian people back home, that the seabed under the Pole, the 1,200-mile-long Lonsomov Ridge, was an extension of Russia's continental shelf. Expedition members were treated like heroes when they came home. "We were there first and we can claim the entire Arctic, but if our neighbors want some part of it, then maybe we can negotiate with them," said Vladimir Zhironovsky, the populist leader of Russia's ultranationalist Liberal Democratic Party.

Be that as it was and continues to be, Canada's last-minute claim to the North Geographic Pole was a bit of a head-scratcher. Either leaders of the Canadian mapping team had concluded that the country's case for claiming the North Pole was weak or they simply didn't have the time, inclination, or funding that was necessary to make Canada's case a strong one. Some people, including me for a brief period, suspected that Harper was pandering, as Putin often does, to public sentiment.

Doubtful as that is, Canada and Russia aren't the only countries guilty of showboating in the Arctic. Denmark's dustup with Canada over Hans Island, a one-half-square-mile chunk of lifeless rock off the coast of Ellesmere Island, has become farcical, with both countries dispatching helicopters and frigates, planting flags, and briefly occupying the island at various times in recent years. A "Free Hans Island" website orchestrated, it seems, by a group calling themselves— tongue-in-cheek, one hopes—the Hans Island Liberation Front, underlines how silly and what a waste of time and money it all is.

Yin Zhuo, a retired Chinese rear admiral, added to the farce a few years ago when he declared that "the Arctic belongs to all the people around the world as no nation has sovereignty over it." Chinese government officials have since tried to distance themselves from that statement, but without much success.

A handful of members of the U.S. Senate haven't acted any better by making it clear that they would oppose repeated attempts by, among others, three U.S. presidents, the U.S. Navy, the U.S. Chamber of Commerce, and the American Petroleum Institute to have UNCLOS ratified. All three presidents knew that they wouldn't get the two-thirds majority that was needed, so they didn't bother trying to push it forward.

Republican senators' success in blocking ratification of UNCLOS is based on myths and misconceptions about how the treaty might infringe on U.S. sovereignty. Although there was some truth to these fears in 1982 when the treaty was originally drafted with influence from the Soviet Union, amendments made in 1994 would now codify U.S. legal rights to exploit oil and gas resources beyond the exclusive economic zone, the maritime area within 200 nautical miles from a country's baseline, to mine minerals in the region and to lay telecommunication cables in the area. Until UNCLOS is acceded to and ratified, says John Bellinger III, adjunct senior fellow for international and national security law at the Council of Foreign Relations, American companies will be reluctant to invest in deep-sea projects.

Investment considerations aside, allowing politics and showboating to trump science and diplomacy is never constructive, especially when so much needs to be done to ensure that the future development of the Arctic does not compromise the environmental and cultural integrity of the region. A great deal still needs to be done to assess the effects of exploration activities on marine mammals that cross international boundaries, the effect that oil spills will have in those ice-covered regions, and the cumulative effects that energy and resource development will have on wildlife and the ecosystems they live in. More also needs to be done on search-and-rescue operations, oil spill cleanup technology, and shipping and possibly future fishing regulations. Ways to resolve the status of the Northwest Passage and settle boundary disputes over Hans Island, the Lincoln Sea, and an energy-rich area in the Beaufort Sea that both Canada and the United States claim need to be found.

Three years ago, U.S. Admiral James G. Stavridis recognized the risks inherent in this process of carving up the polar region when he noted that even though "the disputes in the Arctic have been dealt with peacefully, climate change could alter the equilibrium over the coming years in the race of temptation for exploitation of more readily accessible natural resources."

He added, "The cascading interests and broad implications stemming from the effects of climate change should cause today's global leaders to take stock and unify their efforts to ensure the Arctic remains a zone of co-operation—rather than proceed down the icy slope towards a zone of competition, or worse a zone of conflict."

Stavridis wasn't coy about what it meant for the military. Military forces, he said, have an important role to play in this area, mainly for specialist assistance around commercial and other interests.

That, of course, is just what Greenpeace protesters discovered while attempting to occupy a drilling ship in Greenland in 2011 and a Russian drilling rig two years later. In both cases, Danish and Russian commandos moved in with automatic weapons. In Russia's case, it once again sent a message to the rest of the world that its strategic interests in the Arctic would not be threatened by anyone.

The idea of countries unifying their efforts to deal with Arctic issues is a bold one, coming as it does from a military strategist like Stavridis. It is, however, nothing new. In 1979, University of Toronto political scientist Franklyn Griffiths came up with a proposal that would have set up a demilitarized zone in the Arctic in which polar nations would cooperate in areas of pollution control and scientific study. Lincoln Bloomfield, the former director of Global Issues for the National Security Council in the United States, expanded on that idea with a much broader proposal two years later. Russian President Mikhail Gorbachev gave the concept international credibility in 1987 when he called for a treaty on cooperation in the Arctic.

One model demonstrates how such cooperation can be accomplished. In 1957, scientists from sixty-seven nations joined forces in an attempt to coordinate worldwide measurements of Earth, the oceans, the atmosphere, and the sun. Coming at a time when geopolitical tensions were on the rise, as they are now, the accomplishments of the 1957–1958 International Geophysical Year were extraordinary. Not only did the studies result in the launching of *Sputnik*, the discovery of the Van Allen belts that ring Earth, the charting of ocean depths and currents, and a systematic understanding of Earth's magnetic field, they inspired the signing of the Antarctic Treaty.

Since the signing of that treaty in Washington, D.C., in 1959, fifty countries have become party to a complex framework of agreements that sets aside Antarctica as a scientific preserve, bans military activities, and prohibits resource exploitation. The agreements, known collectively as the Antarctic Treaty System, are the main reason Antarctica is the only continent in the world that has not been the site of a war, a nuclear explosion, or a manmade environmental disaster.

Although the concept of a treaty or an overarching international agreement on the Arctic has been discussed, these discussions have never been able to cut through the complexity of the many issues in the Arctic. Unlike in Antarctica, there are people living north of the Arctic Circle. Nearly two million people live in Russia, 650,000 in Alaska, 130,000 in Canada, and a little more than a million in Greenland, Iceland, the Scandinavian countries, and the Faeroe Islands combined. The cultural and economic interests of these people would have to be represented and accounted for in any future treaty. In addition, many of them, including the Inuit of the Canadian Arctic and Alaska, won a certain degree of self-governing power when they became landowners through various claims processes.

Territorial boundaries in the Arctic have also not been resolved, nor has the status of the Northwest Passage through northern Canada. Canada maintains that the waters within its archipelago are historic internal waters, meaning that not even innocent passage rights of other vessels apply there. In territorial waters, on the other hand, all states have innocent passage rights.

In 2008, Scott G. Borgerson, a fellow at the Council of Foreign Relations, articulated the need for an overarching agreement in the Arctic when he warned in the influential journal *Foreign Affairs* that the United States cannot afford "to stand idly by" and watch as events unfold in the polar world.

"The Arctic region is not currently governed by any comprehensive multilateral norms and regulations because it was never expected to become a navigable waterway or a site for large-scale commercial development," he wrote in the spring of 2008. "Decisions made by Arctic powers in the coming years will therefore profoundly shape the future of the region for decades. Without U.S. leadership to help develop diplomatic solutions to competing claims and potential conflicts, the region could erupt in an armed mad dash for its resources."

Borgerson has since offered up a mea culpa of sorts. Pessimists like him, he acknowledged in 2013, were wrong in suggesting that conflicts could end in "armed brinkmanship." In 2008, he pointed out, Canada, Denmark, Norway, Russia, and the United States issued the Ilulisaat Declaration in which they reaffirmed their support for the Arctic Council and the UNCLOS and vowed to work out overlapping claims in an orderly manner.

The proof of that, in fact, came in 2010 when the United States and Norway settled a boundary dispute in the maritime region of

Svalbard. Canada and the Denmark also appear to making progress on Hans Island, and Arctic countries have come to an agreement on search-and-rescue operations and commercial fishing in some places.

A funny thing has happened since then, though. In 2014, Russia shocked the western world when it sent in forces to wrest control of the Crimean peninsula from Ukraine. In justifying the invasion, Russia accused the United States and the European Union of fomenting the rebellion that resulted in Ukraine's president, Victor Yanukoych, who is widely perceived as a Russian ally, fleeing the country.

Western leaders, including Hillary Clinton, were quick to link Arctic imperatives to the Crimean crisis. Russia has the longest coastline in the Arctic, and Russians "have been aggressively reopening military bases" in the region, she told a Montreal audience in March 2014. The country, she added, recently imprisoned several Greenpeace activists and regularly sends military air flights over parts of Canada and Alaska, "testing our responses. We need a united front."

Remarkably, most experts suggested that this and subsequent attempts to expel Russia from the Group of Eight (G8) nations would not affect future cooperation in the Arctic even as Sweden and Finland seek full membership in the North American Treaty Organization, or NATO. It is hard to believe that Russia would not see Sweden and Finland's inclusion as an act of aggression. With both Sweden and Finland attaining membership in NATO, Norway would likely convince NATO allies to expand the organization's presence on Russia's north flank. Without a say in the G8, Russia could retaliate by vetoing future proposals made by the Arctic Council.

Thordur Aegir Oskarsson, Iceland's ambassador to Canada in 2014, may have said it best when he noted that nothing stays the same and that new lines will be drawn and walls will continue to be rattled. "There is no guarantee," he said, "that the cracks presently detected within the Arctic Circle will not happen again in the future, specifically to arguably the most neglected and also the most sensitive dimension of the Arctic Agenda, the security dimension."

Oskarsson is correct in suggesting that the current rudimentary arrangements of Arctic governance may not be able to handle the challenges that come with commercialization and resource development in the Arctic. Important differences remain over the status of the

Northwest Passage, and there are no effective mechanisms in place to deal with the consequences of oil spilling under ice that is moving from one territory to another. In addition, time will tell if boundary disputes over the North Pole and other places will be resolved. Such areas that may be economically unimportant now could prove to be valuable in the future.

As much needed as an international agreement on managing the Arctic may be, there is no consensus on what an Arctic treaty would look like. Similarly, there is no agreement on whether a treaty or a charter is the best way to manage and protect the economic, environmental, and cultural interests in the polar world.

Oran Young is perhaps the leading scholar on the subject of Arctic governance. Based at the Bren School at the University of California, Santa Barbara, he is also director of the Institute of Arctic Studies and adjunct professor of political science at the University of Tromsø in Norway. No one has been on top of this subject as long as he has, except perhaps Franklyn Griffiths.

Young believes that fears expressed about an environmental crisis unfolding in the Arctic are substantially exaggerated. Although he acknowledges that it is important to consider the possibility of worst-case scenarios unfolding, he discounts the idea of a Wild West–like land rush. Young is not alone in suggesting that the development of oil and gas reserves located beneath the continental shelves of the Arctic beyond the limits of the existing exclusive economic zones is highly unlikely during the foreseeable future. Most experts believe that, for technological and regulatory reasons, efforts to tap offshore oil and gas reserves in the Arctic will focus on energy fields lying well within the limits of exclusive economic zones during the foreseeable future.

Young is confident that issues pertaining to territorial claims and future shipping practices can be dealt with adequately by UNCLOS and the International Maritime Organization, which came into being in 1948 to deal with legal and administrative matters that improve safety as sea. He does concede, however, that there is good reason to reassess current governance arrangements in and for the Arctic in light of what is going on. The solution is not a treaty, he adds, but what he describes as a "somewhat messy patchwork made up of disparate pieces," a soft-law approach that can quickly adapt to rapidly changing circumstances.

"Even if it were feasible, would we want a formally legally binding treaty for the Arctic?" he asked me when we discussed the issue. "There is a tendency to think of formal arrangements like the Antarctic Treaty System, but there are also advantages to having a soft approach in addressing Arctic issues. Unlike treaties that are rigid and take tremendous time and effort, informal agreements can be made more quickly. They can have more substance, and they can provide for greater adaptability. I think it would be a mistake to set out a rigid set of rules now for a future that is very uncertain."

Young holds the majority view in this case. In recent years, the United States, Canada, and, to a lesser extent, the European Union have distanced themselves from the idea of an overarching treaty. Joseph Spears, principal of the Horseshoe Bay Maritime Law Group in Vancouver, believes that they all made the correct decision.

Spears looks at the issue from the view of a legal practitioner who has extensive experience in international maritime law. More than anything else, he says, international shipping requires uniformity. "Arguably the most successful international U.N. agency is the International Maritime Organization [IMO], which has traditionally dealt with shipping matters," he says. "At present, the IMO is developing a polar code to regulate shipping. This is an existing entity that can be used to regulate Arctic shipping. In addition, coastal states such as Canada have enacted far-sighted and strong marine environmental legislation to regulate shipping within the marine jurisdictions."

Even if the IMO succeeds in its push for a polar code, Spears notes, the code would not require coastal states to put in the necessary shipping infrastructure and pollution response capabilities.

Like Young, Spears believes that UNCLOS provides for the development of special areas where new regimes can be put in place. In his view, this strategy is more than sufficient to develop the necessary environmental safeguards. With respect to the seaward extension of the continental shelf, Article 76 of UNCLOS provides the mechanism for delimiting it.

As big as this issue is, the cast of characters in this debate is a small one. Most everyone knows and respects one another. Some have teacher-student relationships.

Clearly, however, a line has been drawn in the sand between

so-called soft approach advocates like Young and Spears and the treaty approach that a new generation of academic and legal scholars like Rob Huebert and Timo Koivurova are advocating.

Huebert is associate director of the Centre for Military and Strategic Studies at the University of Calgary and a member of Canada's Polar Commission. He believes that the soft approach, which relies largely on voluntary cooperation, is insufficient to deal with the challenges that climate change, energy development, and increased shipping will bring to the Arctic.

"Over the past fifteen years," he says, "the Arctic nations have established an initial framework for cooperation in addressing issues of mutual concern in the Arctic. The existing cooperative framework, embodied in the Arctic Council, is characterized by this 'soft law' or essentially voluntary approach, reflecting the lack of appetite of at least some of the Arctic governments for more strenuous treaty arrangements."

Issues, he notes, are generally brought forward for consideration first and foremost as technical issues. As a consequence, priority is placed on scientific research and problem identification rather than on cooperative remedial action. The existing arrangement, he adds, is also a "low-cost" approach, with no permanent secretariat and few real resources for cooperative action.

Huebert believes that without a stronger framework for cooperative management, the living resources of the Arctic are likely to suffer, essential habitat will be degraded, and the traditional subsistence way of life of many Arctic communities will be endangered. The question now, he says, is who is most able to manage and devise such a system: the United Nations, the Arctic Council, or the five coastal Arctic nations—Canada, United States, Russia, Norway, and Denmark—that are in the process of claiming new territory in the Arctic?

The Arctic Council, which was set up in 1996 to provide a means for promoting cooperation, coordination, and interaction among Arctic government states, had a good, short run of it in recent years until the chairmanship was transferred from Norway to Canada in 2013. The council has progressed from simply being a policy-shaping body to an organization that is making policy. It has, to its credit, two Arctic-wide agreements: one on search and rescue and another on prevention of oil spills.

Thus far, however, it has shown no appetite for an Arctic treaty. And, to the surprise of some, it has stalled badly under Canada's chairmanship, with high-profile personnel changes, mixed signals relating to conservation and resource development, and inflammatory remarks and actions from Leona Aglukkaq, Canada's ambassador to the Arctic Council. Her December 2013 Twitter posting of a photo of a freshly killed polar bear with the caption "Enjoy" was at best ill-advised, even though she was resending it from an Inuk who had been boasting of a cousin killing his first bear. Doing so from Moscow, where she was attending the fortieth anniversary of an international agreement on polar bear conservation, also didn't help her image, an image that had suffered by her almost deafening silence on climate change since she had been appointed the government's minister of environment.

Aglukkaq aside, some critics like Koivurova see in the Arctic Council signs of smugness and delusion.

Koivurova is a research professor and the director of the Northern Institute for Environmental and Minority Law, Arctic Centre/University of Lapland. He was also coleader of a global research project on the theory and practice of transboundary environmental impact assessments.

Koivurova believes that one possible way of moving forward quickly is to choose a framework treaty that formalizes the current membership of the Arctic Council, adds certain guiding principles related to environmental protection, and challenges to sustainable development. These changes would shorten the time needed to achieve consensus in negotiations and put legal protocols in place when the time is ripe.

The Arctic Council may not like it, he concedes. If it continues without a legal mandate, however, he fears that there is great danger of it becoming a facade behind which unilateral and uncoordinated development oriented parties of the Arctic states can proceed.

As daunting as the prospects of a treaty are in a world as complicated as the Arctic, Koivurova is confident that the idea is a viable and urgent one.

"This is a region that is undergoing dramatic change," he says. "We know that economic activities are going to enter the region. There is no evidence to suggest that the soft-law approach that we have now will be effective in regulating these activities in the future. What is required is the establishment of regional institutions with legal powers to regulate."

If there have been doubts about how quickly economic and geopolitical developments are taking place in the Arctic, as there were just a few years ago, they were largely dispelled in the spring of 2013 when China—along with Japan, South Korea, Singapore, India, and Italy—was granted observer status in the Arctic Council.

Five or six years ago, most experts would have reacted skeptically to the suggestion that China, for example, would become a major player in the Arctic. In the past few years, however, China has been investing considerable resources to ensure that it will be a major Arctic power in the future. Like other countries now looking northward, it wants to exploit the emerging shipping opportunities and the largely unexploited energy and mineral resources in the region.

China didn't bide its time waiting to hear how its application to the Arctic Council would be decided. In addition to recently signing a free-trade agreement with Iceland, China has built an embassy there as well. To date, Chinese resource companies have invested $400 million in energy and mining projects in Arctic Canada, and they're promising to invest $2.3 billion and three thousand Chinese workers in a mammoth, British-led mining project in Greenland.

What's more, China has increased funding for Arctic research, set up a polar institute in Shanghai, and in 2014 once again sent the Chinese icebreaker *Xue Long* through the Northeast Passage above Russia and Scandinavia, presumably to determine the suitability of using that route as a commercial waterway. It is currently building another icebreaker and planning at least three Arctic expeditions in the future.

Suspicious as some Arctic countries may be of China's ambitions, each one has signaled in its own way that the time for exploiting the Arctic has come. Norwegian and Danish officials said as much at the recent World Economic Forum in Davos, as did Aglukkaq when she assumed chairmanship of the Arctic Council in May 2013. A key focus, she said, "will be on natural resource development in the circumpolar region." Putting an exclamation mark on that, Canada's prime minister has committed $300 million in funding to complete a "Road to Resources" highway, the first in Canada that connects the south to Tuktoyaktuk on the Arctic coast.

The United States has also given the green light to energy development off the coast of Alaska, despite the debacle that characterized Royal Dutch Shell's $4.5 billion effort to drill for oil in the region.

Whichever way one looks at it, the economic exploitation of the Arctic's resources may well be unfolding faster than many experts anticipated five or six years ago. UNCLOS was and still does offer a means of orderly development that complies with international law, but the treaty was signed in 1982 when climate change was not yet on radar. Amendments made in 1994 never considered the ambitions of non-Arctic countries such as China or even the possibility of exploiting energy and mineral resources in this part of the world.

What's more is that recommendations by the U.N. Commission on the Limits of the Continental Shelf are nonbinding. So if, for example, Canada succeeds in this last-minute bid to claim the North Geographic Pole, there is no legal mechanism that compels Russia to accept the recommendation by the U.N. commission. The commission only assesses the science of the submission. UNCLOS then requires that all overlap be peacefully resolved. Countries can do so by negotiating directly, or they can use a system provided by UNCLOS.

Therein lies a question that nobody has dared asked: What would happen if diplomacy failed to resolve that dispute? For instance, what would Canada do if Russia began drilling for oil or mining for minerals around the North Pole? Canada has just six icebreakers, all of which are nearing their end of life. Russia has thirty-seven, six of which are more powerful than Canada's flagship. Would the United States intervene? Similarly, what would the United States do if China started fishing in waters that the United States would legitimately be entitled to when it has not yet acceded to UNCLOS?

A few years ago, I presented the following scenario to reinforce the idea that the Arctic needs to be governed by either a treaty or an overarching form of international agreements. This one is updated here to take into account what has happened in the Arctic since then.

In this case, a foreign ship challenges Canada's sovereignty over the Northwest Passage. Double-hulled and up to the standards that the Canadian government demands, the ship nevertheless runs into thick ice and starts spilling oil into Lancaster Sound just when several thousand narwhals and beluga whales are migrating in from Greenland. At least two dozen polar bears are on a sheet of ice nearby hunting seals, which in turn are preying on arctic cod.

Canada's flagship icebreaker, the *Louis St. Laurent*, has just left port in Halifax and has run into the same computer problems that shut its engines down for four days in the Beaufort Sea in the summer of 2006. The United States can't help because its two aging icebreakers are out of commission and there have been delays in building the new one that was promised.

There are only four helicopters in the region. One is down due to mechanical reasons. Another is grounded because of weather. Airpower from the south is unavailable because most of the planes and helicopters that would normally be available have been deployed to fight forest and tundra fires in Alaska and the Yukon that are bigger than the ones that occurred in 2003, 2007, and 2014.

A storm as big or bigger than the Arctic cyclone of 2012 has formed off the coast of Alaska and is gaining steam, churning up ice as its heads toward the site of the oil spill. Ocean currents carry the oil toward those schools of arctic cod and to Prince Leopold Island, where Arctic birds have successfully reproduced after two years of extreme weather that caused catastrophic nesting failures. Strong winds carry this oil into Baffin Bay and Davis Strait, where Greenlandic ships are fishing for turbot. Thick clouds make it impossible for satellites to track the plume of oil.

Finland and Sweden are now part of NATO. Norway has convinced the organization to expand its presence in the region. NATO does so by conducting exercises along Russia's north flank. Russia is angry and in no mood to cooperate in dealing with a spill that does not affect its territory.

In just a few short days, the *Exxon Valdez* is no longer the worst oil spill to have occurred in the Arctic.

Chapter 11

Conclusion

K IM HOLMÉN IS A TALL, fifty-nine-year-old man with long, thinning white hair and a scraggly gray beard. The dark sunglasses he wears outside make him look more like a member of the American blues and rock group ZZ Top than the international director of the Norwegian Polar Institute. The beard, he told me when we first met, grew from a bet he had made ten years earlier with a machinist working at Ny-Ålesund, an international research center that the Norwegians oversee on the island of Spitsbergen. The bet was over who could grow the longest one.

"Who won?" I asked as he and I stood on the Kongsvegen Glacier watching American glaciologist Jack Kohler drill into the ice.

"Nobody yet," he said as he stroked his beard.[1]

The snowmobile trip from Ny-Ålesund to the Kongsvegen Glacier is an hour-long ride along a razor-thin coastal plain that straddles the mountains and massive ice fields of Spitsbergen in the Norwegian archipelago of Svalbard. It's a relatively easy ride except for one small section where the route narrows dramatically between two cliffs that separate the snow-covered mountains on one side of the fiord from the icy sea on the other.

Minutes before we set off that day, Kohler advised me to "really lean uphill" toward the cliff on the mountainside as I passed through this squeeze. Otherwise, he said, I might slide down the slope and fall over the cliff straight into the water.

"It's not as bad as it sounds," he added. "Besides, you're Canadian. You guys snowmobile every day, don't you?"

Kohler looked at me and I looked at him without offering comment. I wasn't sure whether he was serious or just pulling my leg, but given the possibility that he might think twice about having me along to watch as he drilled a core into the heart of the glacier, I thought it best not to tell him that I hadn't mounted a snowmobile in two years.

It had been four days since I arrived in Svalbard. In that time, I got to spend some time with Kohler on the glacier, with German divers on the coast, and with Italian scientists who served up wonderfully strong coffee that was not to be found anywhere in Ny-Ålesund, a former coal mining town that is home to only forty people year-round. Holmén also took me up a gondola to the Zeppelin Observatory, which is located on a steep mountainside outside of Ny-Ålesund. The observatory, which is generally off-limits to outsiders because of the risk of contaminating its sensors, offers a rare platform for scientists to monitor global atmospheric change and the long-range transportation of pollutants high above the inversion layer and far from human pollution.

Even then, I was having trouble figuring out what to make of this scientific melting pot. Most of the visitors to Ny-Ålesund are, like Kohler, foreigners. The German, French, and Chinese scientists are here pretty much year-round with the Norwegians. The Japanese had left the day I arrived. Some of the Italians were packing up to go. The Dutch, the British, the Koreans, and the scientists from India would be here for the summer, as would an American crew that was planning to come in. Even Holmén, I was surprised to learn, was Swedish.

Each one, I learned during my time there, brings something from home, be it food, drink, coffees, teas, language, or attitudes as well as research protocols and priorities that set them apart. In nearly every case, Norway's interests in the Arctic are not uppermost on their minds.

When they all come together in the dining room to eat three times a day—whenever they're not out in the field, that is—there is, however, a clear sense that they are here for a common purpose: to study atmospheric phenomena and the changing Arctic ecosystem (Figure 11.1).

Compared with other Arctic nations, Norway's management of its polar world has been progressive and occasionally visionary. Since 1973, the Norwegian government has established twenty-nine protected areas: seven national parks, six nature reserves, fifteen bird sanctuaries, and one additional park designed to protect the geology of an island. Altogether, these protected areas make up 15,400 square miles, or 65 percent of the land mass. Nearly all of Svalbard's territorial waters—86.5 percent—are under some form of protection. The Kong Karls Land Archipelago, an important breeding ground for polar bears in Svalbard and Franz Josef Land, is completely off-limits to all visitors. Scientists who study the animals are allowed to go there only on a limited basis.

Norway's generous facilitation of international research in its own backyard was inspired in part by the 1920 Svalbard Treaty that gave the country sovereignty over the archipelago. In addition to obliging Norway to preserve the natural environment of the region, the treaty prohibits the establishment of military fortifications anywhere in the area.

The Norwegians have adhered to the spirit of the treaty, if not its exact wording. The treaty provides no specific rules for scientific research, for example, but Norway has given almost every country the right to set up a scientific field station at Ny-Ålesund as long as the countries are willing to pay rent and follow some basic rules. Today, ten countries operate fourteen research stations in the archipelago. In any given year, as many as a thousand scientists will pass through. The rent they pay does not come close to covering the costs associated with running the facilities, which include everything from a state-of-the-art marine laboratory and a diver decompression tank to a liquid nitrogen maker.

The government of Norway spends about 1.4 billion Norwegian krones annually on polar science. The lion's share—80 to 90 percent—is spent in the Arctic. For all the excellent scientific data collected and the scientists' awareness of issues and concerns, however, the rapid warming of the Arctic has not been halted by any of the research that

Figure 11.1 Glaciologist Jack Kohler prepares to drill into the Kongsvegen Glacier near Ny-Ålesund, an international research center that the Norwegians oversee on the island of Spitsbergen. Photo credit: Edward Struzik

has been done thus far. Winters, according to Holmén, are warmer than they've ever been. As a consequence, the western fiords have not iced over in several years. Mackerel, Atlantic cod, and other more southerly species have been moving in to take advantage of warmer waters that may not be favorable to the region's arctic cod and arctic char.

The glaciers that Kohler and other scientists have been monitoring have been retreating just as fast as others throughout the polar world. Like North America's caribou, Svalbard's reindeer are struggling, as are its three thousand polar bears. In 2014, the proportion of female polar bears giving birth to cubs in one small part of Svalbard crashed to an historic low. Jon Aars and his colleagues at the Norwegian Polar Institute discovered that only three of the twenty-nine adult female bears they were tracking produced cubs. They had expected the number to be at least nine or ten, which is still about five short of the typical number of bears that would have given birth thirty years ago.

The Norwegian government, however, hasn't been standing idly by as this tsunami of climate-related events takes over its ability to do something about it. Norway prohibits energy companies from drilling in the protected areas or where ice presents a hazard. The farming of fish in Svalbard is prohibited. Starting in 2015, tour ships and other vessels using heavy oil will not be allowed anywhere near the protected areas, not only because of the threat of a spill, but because of the soot emitted from these types of engines.

Although there is much to praise, Norway's management of Svalbard is not perfect. In 2014, a new coal mine was opened south of Longyearbyen, the main Norwegian settlement on Svalbard, amid parliamentary debates over investing the country's sovereign wealth fund—estimated to be $900 billion—in coal mines around the world. The accidental discovery of shale gas in Svalbard in 2013 has raised the remote possibility of fracking in some parts of the unprotected archipelago as well.

Still, as I traveled through Canada, Alaska, and Arctic Russia after my trip to Svalbard, I was struck by the contrasts between Norway and the manner in which the rest of the world manages and views the Arctic. In Canada, one resource mining company, which had two Canadian senators on its board of directors, had announced plans to build a giant coal mine on the Fosheim Peninsula on Ellesmere Island where Mary Dawson, Richard Harington, and other paleontologists had unearthed the fossils of an ancient Arctic world. Around that same time, the federal government announced plans to shut down the Canadian Foundation for Climate and Atmospheric Sciences. Funding from the foundation was critical to scientists such as those who run a research station on Ellesmere Island similar to the Zeppelin Observatory in Svalbard. While the Inuit of the eastern Arctic were going to court to stop seismic drilling in Lancaster Sound, the Dene in the western Arctic were grappling with a proposal from ConocoPhilips to begin hydraulic fracturing, or fracking, in the Mackenzie River valley just south of the Arctic Circle.

The outlook for the Arctic's future seemed to be no better in Alaska. In 2011, the State of Alaska and several energy companies went to court claiming that the federal government's designation of critical habitat for polar bears in the Bering and Chukchi Seas was excessive. They won that case. Despite Shell's near disastrous mishaps in the Arctic in 2012, the state followed with another lawsuit. This one was against the U.S. Fish and Wildlife Service, the Department of the Interior, claiming that they wrongfully rejected the state's application to look for oil and gas on the coastal plain of the Arctic National Wildlife Refuge.

In Russia, reindeer herders in the Khanty-Mansiysk Autonomous Okrug of western Russia continued to struggle to stop oil and gas companies from drilling in the last 10 percent of wilderness that had not yet been carved up by development. Meanwhile, their Nenet neighbors in the Yamal region were pleading for support after some twelve thousand of their reindeer starved to death during severe icing events in 2014.

Since satellites began providing sea ice data in 1979, the extent of sea ice in the Arctic has declined at an annual rate of 4 percent. This decline has accelerated since 1998—an extremely hot El Niño year—with several seasons of record-breaking losses. The sea ice recovery in 2013 that climate change skeptics like to point to was short-lived and relatively insignificant. In September 2013, sea ice coverage at its minimum was nearly 700,000 square miles less than the historical 1979–2000 average, a difference, the Environmental Protection Agency notes, that is more than twice the size of Texas.

Ten years ago, no one anticipated that sea ice in the Arctic would retreat so rapidly. Now, though, even the most conservative modelers suggest that the Arctic will be seasonally ice-free by 2030, two decades sooner than some of them had predicted just a few years ago.

With these climactic changes come surprises that scientists did not see coming. The Arctic cyclone of 2012 was a big surprise. So were the storm surges that swept into the Yukon-Kuskokwim delta in Alaska in 2005, 2006, and 2011, resulting in flooding that extended, respectively, 30.3 kilometers, 27.4 kilometers, and 32.3 kilometers inland. In 2010, an ice shelf measuring 100 square miles broke off the Petermann Glacier in Greenland, reducing its volume by about 10 percent almost instantly.[2] Another 50-square-mile chunk of ice broke off two years later. Arctic scientists have been surprised so often over the past fifteen years that some of them say that they will be surprised if there are no more surprises in the future.

To be fair, scientists correctly predicted the decline of polar bears in the western Arctic and southern Beaufort Sea as early as the 1990s (Figure 11.2), but few of them saw caribou populations collapsing as catastrophically as they have throughout the circumpolar world in recent years. Likewise, fisheries biologists suspected that Pacific salmon might enter the Arctic along with other Bering Sea species that are migrating north with the receding ice. Not one of them, however, dreamed that Pacific salmon would be caught in Greenland waters and in the eastern Arctic of Canada, as they were in 2012.

Among the most sobering of surprises were the forest and tundra fires that torched vast regions of Arctic Russia, Alaska, and the Yukon and Northwest Territories in the last decade. Four of those years produced some of the worst fires in modern times as well as noxious emissions that migrated thousands of miles south.

The surprises haven't all been bad, though. Wood bison appear to be making a remarkably successful comeback in the Yukon. That's a good sign for Alaska, which plans to reintroduce the species to the wild in 2015. It appears that musk oxen are doing well, as are barren-ground grizzlies, which are expanding northward onto the Arctic islands and eastward toward Hudson Bay and northern Manitoba. There continue to be signs that big cats, like the cougar, might stage a comeback in a region where they have been absent for more than 12,500 years.

Progress toward responsible management of this new Arctic ecosystem is also being made on a number of geopolitical fronts. The process of mapping new boundaries in the unclaimed regions of the Arctic has progressed reasonably well under the auspices of the United Nations Convention on the Law of the Sea. Arctic countries have also agreed not to fish in many of those unclaimed areas.

New questions about the future of the Arctic keep mounting even as many of the old questions are left unanswered, however. No one knows, for example, how the crisis in Ukraine will affect future security and cooperation issues in the Arctic.

Scientists also do not know what will happen if, for example, a disease such as phocine distemper, which is common in midlatitudes, gets a foothold in the Arctic, where narwhal and beluga whales have little or no immunity. The recent discovery of microplastics in the

Figure 11.2 In the 1990s, scientists such as Ian Stirling and Andrew Derocher predicted that polar bear populations at the southern edge of their range would decline as sea ice retreated. Photo credit: Edward Struzik

Arctic Sea raises yet another possibility that Arctic birds, fish, and mammals are ingesting copious amounts of the world's discarded chemicals. Similarly, will the northward migration of marine mammals and fish from the North Pacific Ocean and Bering Sea extend into the Chukchi and Beaufort Seas with any degree of success?

Although geopolitical and climate change effects themselves are complicated, combining them with effects of offshore oil and gas development may well make things more problematic, particularly if this resource extraction accelerates with receding ice cover as some experts suggest it will. In July 2014, World Wildlife Canada released an independent report that concluded that in the event of a major blowout in the Beaufort Sea where Imperial Oil and Chevron have plans to drill the deepest well ever in the Arctic, high winds and powerful currents would cause the oil to spread rapidly. According to the report, the probability of this oil reaching the shores of the calving grounds of the Porcupine caribou in the Arctic National Wildlife Refuge are high.

The use of chemical dispersants to clean up the oil would result in toxic concentrations of dissolved oil entering the water column of the Beaufort Sea where both Arctic char and, increasingly, Pacific salmon are found along with bowheads and beluga whales. If the oil got under the ice, it would be impossible to clean it up.

From his vantage point as international director of the Norwegian Polar Institute, Kim Holmén has watched with exasperation as frontier energy exploration and climate change events continue to overtake the world's ability to do anything meaningful about them. He has no doubt that there will be more surprises from the changes that are currently unfolding.

Holmén cites Bert Bolin, who played a central role in the formation and management of the Intergovernmental Panel on Climate Change, as his mentor. Like Bolin, Holmén doesn't pretend that he has all the answers to the questions about the Arctic's future. "I remember asking Bert once how many original ideas he had come up with during his long career," he says. "Bert thought about this for a moment and then said, 'Three and a half.'"

Holmén's point, of course, is that no one person is going to come up with an idea that will answer all the questions about the future of the Arctic. That's why he believes that the scientific community needs to play a bigger role in telling the world what is happening in the Arctic and why the public should care, as some scientists did in September 2014 when three hundred thousand people marched in New York City and around the world to urge governments to support an agreement to reduce emissions of greenhouse gas emissions. "We need a bigger debate about what state nature should be in a hundred years from now; the Arctic is one of the most important examples of how humankind is altering the state of nature on Earth. We need to understand what is happening and make it known," Holmén says.

Finding ways of adapting to the changes, he added, is also the key to the future. "I just got back from a two-week trip around Greenland," he told me when we last communicated in late July 2014. "There was a lot of discussion about 'new opportunities' when I met with government officials, an example being a growing mackerel fishery in the southeastern waters of Greenland. Regardless of what we do, the changes already inflicted on the atmosphere have committed us to further change in the coming decades. Whether we like it or not, adaptation must be part of our future relation with climate change."

Holmén's comments prompted me to think about the future a little differently. Energy companies with plans in the Arctic tend to prevail because they know what they want and they have the resources to help them get it. The rest of the world—scientists, environmentalists, aboriginal leaders, and the like—haven't reached, and may never reach, a consensus about how to adapt and respond to this future that is unfolding rapidly.

This dichotomy of thought was articulated very bluntly by Frank Pokiak, the chairman of the Inuvialuit Game Council in Arctic Canada. When asked about the July 2014 World Wildlife Canada report on oil spills in the Arctic, he conceded that it would be devastating to his people in the western Arctic of Canada if a spill occurred. In the same breath, however, he acknowledged that the Inuvialuit had not come to a decision on where they stand on offshore oil and gas.

Part of the reason is that they don't have the answers to many of the questions that continue to unfold, as Henry Huntington, Jennifer Francis, and other scientists pointed out in their 2014 U.S. National Academy of Sciences report on emerging questions in the Arctic.

In some ways, this debate about a future Arctic is an old one for Oran Young, a renowned Arctic expert and world leader in the field of international governance and environmental institutions at the Bren School of Environmental Science and Management at the University of California, Santa Barbara. Over the course of more than fifty years, Young has explored ways of using science, traditional knowledge, and institutional frameworks to foster international cooperation in dealing with existing and emerging Arctic issues. He has spent years thinking about how we might shape the future Arctic, giving consideration to everything from putting the Arctic Council in the driver's seat to the merits of creating an Arctic treaty.

Young, however, is now looking at the future of the Arctic differently.

"It's possible that we've devoted too much attention to big glitzy global visions, like the Northern Sea Route as a serious competitor to Suez or Panama or the scramble to extract resources on the scale suggested by the 2008 [U.S. Geological Survey] projections," he says.

"What we may need to think about is the Arctic as a laboratory for exploring transitions to sustainability in settings that are small scale, but heavily impacted by the problems of the consequences of climate change."

The gist of Young's thinking is that offshore oil and gas development and shipping in the Arctic are not happening nearly as quickly as economists predicted but that climate change, on the other hand, is. The best way to move forward, he believes, is to invest in small-scale initiatives that will bring scientists, aboriginal people, decision makers, and various northern interests together to address immediate threats such as forest and tundra fires, sea-level rise, coastal erosion, wildlife population declines, invasive species, and resource development. Such initiatives might, for example, convince both decision makers and the people of Shishmaref in Alaska to relocate rather than spend enormous amounts of money shoring up the community. The lessons learned from Shishmaref, in turn, could then be used as a model for other coastal communities experiencing similar problems.

Following this train of thought, the same small-scale initiative might be applied to the town of Churchill, whose fortunes are tied to the tourists who come to the community each year to watch polar bears migrating through. Experimental efforts to feed starving polar bears in the off-ice season in the future may point the way to saving other polar bear populations. In addition, a better understanding of the effects of shipping out of the port of Churchill might help decide whether it's worth transporting Alberta's bitumen to market sometime in the future, as has been suggested.

As much as this approach makes sense, finding funding for such initiatives will be difficult, especially in Canada where the Conservative government of Prime Minister Stephen Harper has been hostile to climate change debates, toward scientists, and toward most environmental initiatives. The Age of the Arctic may well be here, as Oran Young and Gail Osherenko predicted in a book they cowrote many years ago, but decision makers like Harper and Vladimir Putin see in that only the opportunity to exploit it.

In addition to these small-scale initiatives, what the Arctic really needs is more of the international cooperation that Norway fosters in Ny-Ålesund. The role of the Arctic Council needs to be strengthened.

The case for an Arctic treaty may not be a strong one, but it is a way to debate the issues.

Paul Arthur Berkman is an oceanographer who, along with Oran Young and others at the Bren School, is working on interdisciplinary connections between science, policy, and information technology with regard to cooperative international governance of the Arctic Ocean. He believes that we need both a forum and leadership to foster lasting stability in the Arctic. Looking ahead to 2016 when the Arctic Council celebrates its twentieth anniversary, Berkman sees an opportunity for U.S. President Barack Obama to convene a meeting with all other Arctic heads of state and "act as a statesman who puts out the brushfires of the moment while planting seeds of hope and inspiration for the future.

"The challenge," he says, "is to create a process of ongoing and inclusive dialogue about Arctic issues that have so far eluded shared consideration. With the Arctic, Obama must be brave enough to share the 'coin of peace,' promoting cooperation on one side and preventing conflict on the other."

Perhaps the fastest way of getting to where we need to go lies in the ability of scientists like meteorologist Jennifer Francis to make the connection between severe meteorological events that are increasingly taking their toll down at midlatitudes to the changes that are occurring in the Arctic. A choking pall of smoke from a forest or tundra fire in the Arctic and sub-Arctic regions may well catch the attention of the majority of the population in the south that knows nothing about what's happening in the north. For example, another storm surge such as the one that flooded parts of New York and New Jersey in 2012's Hurricane Sandy almost certainly would get major media coverage if it were tied to changes in the jet stream.

We have already gotten brief glimpses that what happens in the Arctic in the future will matter to the rest of the world, but unless more people understand these connections as more than the occasional deadly storm or air-quality alert day, decision makers will not invest in a road map to a future Arctic that has the best chance of creating some kind of resilient ecosystem. Scientific understanding is critical to this step.

If, however, scientists and the aboriginal people of the north are not given the resources to answer both the questions currently left unanswered and those that will emerge in the future, we in the south will continue to be surprised and punished by events that originate in the future Arctic.

Figuring out what the future will look like in an Arctic world that is constantly changing with each year that passes may appear to be folly, especially when there are 121,000 pieces to the puzzle. These pieces include the cold-climate mammals, birds, fish, invertebrates, plants, and fungi that we know a lot about as well as the microbes and endoparasites that remain largely a mystery. Set against a backdrop of boreal forest, tundra, permafrost, polar deserts, glaciers, ice caps, mountains, rivers, deltas, sea ice, polynyas, gyres, and open ocean, the challenge is even more daunting, but failing to form future Arctic assessments could have consequences, as energy companies have discovered several times in the past thirty-five years in their failed efforts to build multibillion-dollar pipelines through Alaska and the Yukon and Northwest Territories. In each case, the science, the economics, and the cultural interests of aboriginal people in the region were not fully taken into account.

During the 2007–2009 International Polar Year (IPY) that was sponsored by the World Meteorological Organization and the International Council for Science, sixty-two countries spent hundreds of millions of dollars to send thousands of scientists to the polar regions to examine a wide range of physical, biological, and social research topics.

IPY science summed up what we know about the Arctic. In addition to the small-scale initiatives that Young recommends, what's needed now is a similar mechanism—namely, a follow-up to IPY, which some suggest should be called the International Polar Decade—that transforms this knowledge into action. Ideally, this international forum will bring scientists, aboriginal people, industry representatives, and decision makers together to draw a road map to the future. Structured properly, it will result in small-scale local initiatives that address immediate threats such as forest and tundra fires, sea-level rise, coastal erosion, wildlife population declines, invasive species, resource development, commercial shipping, and the possibility of an oil spill. Theoretically, the solutions that come from these local initiatives would be shared with decision makers throughout the polar world.

The so-called Age of the Arctic may well be here, but unless action is taken soon, there will continue to be surprises for which we are not prepared.

Notes

1. When the machinist passed away shortly after from a sudden illness, Holmén decided to keep the beard as a token of friendship and in his memory.

2. To be fair, glaciologist Jason Box saw it coming, but few people believed that it would happen.

Acknowledgments

This book owes a great deal to the scientists, the Inuit, and the Dene who invited me to participate in their Arctic field expeditions and hunting trips in recent years. The list is a long one, but several stand out for reasons that will be obvious to readers. They include the month-long trip I did with John England on Banks Island, my time with Benoit Beauchamp and Steve Grasby on Ellesmere and Axel Heiberg Islands, the very cold week I spent with the Canadian government's mapping team off the coast of Borden Island, the polar bear surveys I did with Ian Stirling and with Darryl Hedman and Vicki Trim, the bison survey I did with Yukon biologist Tom Jung, two sailing trips through the Northwest Passage with oceanographer Eddy Carmack and his colleagues, and another much smaller trip that the World Wildlife Canada organized in the summer of 2012. I would be remiss if I didn't mention the opportunities that paleontologist Richard Harington and paleobotanist James Basinger had offered me in the more distant past when they allowed me to participate in excavations at Strathcona Fiord on Ellesmere Island and at the fossil forest site on Axel Heiberg Island.

Thanks goes as well to the U.S. National Parks Service officials who invited me to come along on a trip to Chukotka with Eva Menadelook, a native of Little Diomede in the Bering Sea, and with Rose Fosdick, vice president of a native Alaskan organization that represents nineteen other small coastal villages in the Bering Strait. The same thanks goes to Kim Holmén of the Norwegian Polar Institute who made my stay in Ny-Ålesund such an eye-opening experience and to the folks at the Canadian Polar Shelf Project in Resolute who have, over the course of more than thirty years, helped me hitchhike my way through the Arctic in a most unorthodox manner. Many of those so-called trips into scientific camps couldn't have been done without the help of director Marty Bergmann, who tragically died in a plane crash en route to Resolute in August 2011. He was, by then, a good friend, a great scientist, and without a doubt unparalleled in his ability to charm, to inform, and to make things happen. I still miss those late-night calls when he'd start off by asking me what I was up to the following summer.

I was also given several other opportunities that helped me write this book in ways that I couldn't have imagined at the time. Danielle Labonté, the former director general of the Canadian Department of Indian Affairs and Northern Development, invited me to be on a selection committee she chaired for the International Polar Year (IPY) conference that was held in Montreal in 2012. Peter Harrison, the chair of the IPY, invited me to be the rapporteur for the Canada/United Kingdom Colloquium on the Arctic that was held in Iqaluit. Peter also asked me to sit in for him at the meeting of the International Collaboration and Cooperation in Arctic Science in Fairbanks, Alaska, in 2011. It was there that I got to sit down and brainstorm with scientists, social scientists, and Arctic directors from the United States, Canada, Norway, Denmark, France, the Netherlands, and South Korea and with representatives from the Aleutian/Pribilof Islands Association. The report we produced on planning for the future Arctic was most instructive.

Several people reviewed parts of this book and offered insights. The list flatters me. They include oceanographer Eddy Carmack, polar bear scientist Andrew Derocher, fire expert Mike Flannigan, peregrine scientist Alastair Franke, caribou biologist Anne Gunn, Jim Leafloor of the Canadian Wildlife Service, limnologist and hydrologist Lance Lesack, Arctic ecologist Mark Mallory, environmental scientist Stewart Rood, Alaska biologist David Tallmon, paleontologist Grant Zazula, Yukon biologist Tom Jung, and political scientists Rob Huebert, Timo Koivurova, and Oran Young. Kim Holmén, international director of the Norwegian Polar Institute, also advised me on one chapter, as did Arctic legal expert Joseph Spears on another. I am also indebted to Henry Huntington and Marilyn Heiman of the Pew Charitable Trusts for offering insights and suggestions. Henry was cochair of the U.S. National Research Council committee that examined emerging research questions in the Arctic and produced a report in 2014. Marilyn directs Pew's work to protect the U.S. Arctic Ocean and its marine life from rapid industrialization made possible by the warming climate and the melting ice cap.

Working with Courtney Lix, the multitalented editor at Island Press, was a pleasure. Courtney gently but very firmly pointed me in the right direction whenever I began swerving off course. Miraculously, I never felt bad when she proved that I might be wrong on more than one occasion. Thanks go as well to my agent Lisa Adams of the Garamond Agency who set things up and stood by constantly offering a helping hand. I can't thank my wife, Julie, and my children, Sigrid and Jacob, to whom I dedicate this book, enough for being patient and understanding and for putting up with my long absences. Finally, I will always be indebted to my dog, Maggie, who reminded me constantly that it was unhealthy to sit at a desk for ten hours a day without taking at least three walks.

About the Author

Edward Struzik has lived in and has spent the better of the past thirty-five years exploring the circumpolar Arctic by foot, ski, dog team, bush plane, helicopter, canoe, kayak, sailboat, and icebreaker. He is a regular contributing writer for *Yale Environment 360*, and his articles, essays, research reports, and photographs have also appeared in dozens of magazines, journals, and university publications around the world, including *Foreign Policy Review*, *Policy Options*, *World Policy Blog*, *Conservation Biology*, *Canadian Geographic*, *International Wildlife*, *Geo (Russia)*, and *Equinox Explore* as well as for the Program on Water Issues at the Munk School of Global Affairs at the University of Toronto.

In addition to a citation of merit for the Grantham Prize for Excellence in Reporting on the Environment, Struzik has received the prestigious Atkinson Fellowship in Public Policy, the Michener Deacon Fellowship in Public Policy, the Roland Michener Award for Meritorious Public Service in Journalism, and the Sir Sandford Fleming Medal, awarded by the Royal Canadian Institute, Canada's oldest scientific society, for outstanding contributions to the understanding of science.

Struzik has been a Knight Science Journalism Fellow at the Massachusetts Institute of Technology, a Southam Fellow at the University of Toronto, and rapporteur for the Canada/United Kingdom Colloquium on the Arctic and Northern Dimensions in World Issues. He is currently a fellow at the School of Policy Studies, Queen's Institute for Energy and Environmental Policy at Queen University in Kingston, Canada. He lives in Edmonton, Alberta, close to the Rocky Mountains where he often hikes and skis with his wife, Julia; his children, Jacob and Sigrid; his dog, Maggie; and friends and scientists.